Managing Social Anxiety

Managing Social Anxiety

A COGNITIVE-BEHAVIORAL THERAPY APPROACH

SECOND EDITION

Therapist Guide

Debra A. Hope • Richard G. Heimberg •
Cynthia L. Turk

OXFORD
UNIVERSITY PRESS

2010

OXFORD

UNIVERSITY PRESS

Oxford University Press, Inc., publishes works that further
Oxford University's objective of excellence
in research, scholarship, and education.

Oxford   New York
Auckland   Cape Town   Dar es Salaam   Hong Kong   Karachi
Kuala Lumpur   Madrid   Melbourne   Mexico City   Nairobi
New Delhi   Shanghai   Taipei   Toronto

With offices in
Argentina   Austria   Brazil   Chile   Czech Republic   France   Greece
Guatemala   Hungary   Italy   Japan   Poland   Portugal   Singapore
South Korea   Switzerland   Thailand   Turkey   Ukraine   Vietnam

Copyright © 2010 by Oxford University Press, Inc.

Published by Oxford University Press, Inc.
198 Madison Avenue, New York, New York 10016

www.oup.com

Oxford is a registered trademark of Oxford University Press

Library of Congress Cataloging-in-Publication Data

Hope, Debra A.
    Managing social anxiety : a cognitive-behavioral therapy approach : therapist guide / Debra A. Hope, Richard G. Heimberg,
Cynthia L. Turk. — 2nd ed.
        p.   ;   cm. — (TreatmentsThatWork)
    Includes bibliographical references.
    ISBN 978-0-19-533668-9
    1. Anxiety—Treatment.   2. Anxiety—Social aspects.   3. Cognitive therapy.   I. Heimberg, Richard G.
II. Turk, Cynthia L.   III. Title.   IV. Series: Treatments that work.
    [DNLM: 1. Phobic Disorders—therapy.   2. Cognitive Therapy—methods.   3. Shyness.   WM 178 H791m 2010]
    RC531.H67 2010
    616.85'2206—dc22

                                                                                                2009050848

9   8   7   6   5   4   3   2   1

Printed in the United States of America
on acid-free paper

About Treatments *ThatWork*™

Stunning developments have taken place in healthcare over the last several years, but many of our widely accepted interventions and strategies in mental health and behavioral medicine have been brought into question by research evidence as not only lacking benefit, but perhaps, inducing harm. Other strategies have been proven effective using the best current standards of evidence, resulting in broad-based recommendations to make these practices more available to the public. Several recent developments are behind this revolution. First, we have arrived at a much deeper understanding of pathology, both psychological and physical, which has led to the development of new, more precisely targeted interventions. Second, our research methodologies have improved substantially, such that we have reduced threats to internal and external validity, making the outcomes more directly applicable to clinical situations. Third, governments around the world and healthcare systems and policymakers have decided that the quality of care should improve, that it should be evidence-based, and that it is in public's interest to ensure that this happens (Barlow, 2004; Institute of Medicine, 2001).

Of course, the major stumbling block for clinicians everywhere is the accessibility of newly developed evidence-based psychological interventions. Workshops and books can go only so far in acquainting responsible and conscientious practitioners with the latest behavioral healthcare practices and their applicability to individual patients. This new series, Treatments *ThatWork*™, is devoted to communicating these exciting new interventions to clinicians on the frontlines of practice.

The manuals and workbooks in this series contain step-by-step detailed procedures for assessing and treating specific problems and diagnoses. But this series also goes beyond the books and manuals by providing ancillary materials that will approximate the supervisory process in assisting practitioners in the implementation of these procedures in their practice.

In our emerging healthcare system, the growing consensus is that evidence-based practice offers the most responsible course of action for the mental health professional. All behavioral healthcare clinicians deeply desire to provide the best possible care for their patients. In this series, our aim is to close the dissemination and information gap and make that possible.

The second edition of this therapist guide is designed to give mental health professionals the necessary tools to assess and treat social anxiety disorder. Although the components of the program remain unchanged, the authors have updated the guide to include clearer instructions for facilitating treatment, specifically for conducting in-session exposures and cognitive restructuring exercises. Also provided is helpful information for structuring treatment including suggested number of sessions for each chapter, session outlines, lists of materials needed, and homework assignments.

Clinicians will find this guide comprehensive and easy to use. It has everything you need to implement a clinically proven and scientifically sound treatment for social anxiety.

David H. Barlow, Editor-in-Chief,
Treatments *ThatWork*™
Boston, MA

References

Barlow, D. H. (2004). Psychological treatments. *American Psychologist, 59,* 869–878.

Institute of Medicine. (2001). *Crossing the quality chasm: A new health system for the 21st century.* Washington, DC: National Academy Press.

Preface

We are pleased to present to you the second edition of our Therapist Guide to the updated second edition of the client workbook titled *Managing Social Anxiety: A Cognitive Behavioral Approach.* We have endeavored to update the procedures and background to reflect current science and clinical work in the psychopathology and treatment of social anxiety while preserving the core therapy approach that has demonstrated success across many clinical trials. Over the years, we have been gratified by the positive response we have received from clinicians who have utilized this approach with their clients. We have also listened carefully to feedback from many people about ways the manuals could be improved. We appreciate this feedback and hope that we have incorporated the best of it into the new edition.

The first three chapters of the therapist guide have been extensively updated to reflect the current literature on social anxiety disorder. This will provide the newest background information for therapists. The assessment recommendations have been updated as well. Some newer measures are discussed but the core pretreatment self-report assessment remains the same. Because we believe that few therapists outside of research centers are able to employ formal behavioral tests, we have updated these recommendations to reflect procedures for behavioral assessment that are feasible in all practice settings. These changes were informed by our own private practice work, and we hope they provide a good balance of gathering crucial behavioral data that avoid the biases of self-report with an efficient assessment strategy.

In chapter 4 of this therapist guide in which we provide an overview of the treatment approach, we have made a number of changes that we think therapists will find useful. We have included a table that outlines what we typically cover in a 16-session treatment program, including the in-session procedures, homework, and reading from the client workbook. Additional material on working with clients who do not share the same first language as the therapist and clients who identify as gay, lesbian, or bisexual has also been added. Both of these changes reflect our own experiences providing the treatment or in clinical supervision as well as recent excellent research on the presentation of social anxiety among sexual minorities.

Because the three authors of the therapist guide and the client workbook practice and supervise across fairly different settings, we particularly attended to difficulties in understanding or implementing the procedures across all of our settings since the publication of the first edition. Several of these involved execution of in-session exposure and implementation of the cognitive restructuring exercises. Thus, we have made numerous small changes in procedures and instructions to better clarify how we intend the treatment to be implemented.

The most dramatic change in the treatment procedures themselves is that we have replaced the extensive session-by-session self-monitoring procedures with a new session change measure. We thought that the self-monitoring was burdensome, and the data were not as informative in treatment as they could be. The new measure is more efficient and will help track client change, an essential feature of this therapy and all evidence-based practice.

We have made a number of changes in the early psychoeducational sessions. A section and worksheet on using motivational interviewing to help enhance motivation to change social anxiety appears in the first therapy session. This addition reflects recent evidence that motivational enhancement can be an important adjunct to exposure-based interventions for anxiety disorders. We have moved the construction of the Fear and Avoidance Hierarchy to an earlier session as feedback from therapists suggested it would be useful in building rapport. It also allows therapists to understand a client's idiographic presentation, which should facilitate earlier conceptualization of the case. A detailed discussion of cognitive features of social anxiety that many clients found difficult and was not essential to the treatment rationale was moved from the client workbook to the therapist guide. Therapists can now use this information in sessions as they see fit. There are also numerous other changes in which specific exercises and examples that did not seem to work well with a significant number of clients were modified. Lastly, the therapist guide provides more specific advice regarding helping the client to get repeated practice monitoring cognitions in these early sessions and giving feedback on homework that is likely to facilitate the client's ability to work with cognitions later, during cognitive restructuring, and, even later, when challenging core beliefs.

Material for the two sessions devoted to cognitive restructuring has been updated to some extent. However, the biggest change in this section is that some material previously covered in the second session has been moved to the first cognitive session. This shift should allow a better balance of content between sessions and allow more time for practicing cognitive restructuring procedures in the second cognitive session.

The Be Your Own Cognitive Coach (BYOCC) Worksheet, which was the backbone of the homework assignments for exposures, has been updated and renamed Be Your Own Cognitive Therapist (BYOCT). These changes reflect increased scientific evidence of the importance of post-event processing in social anxiety. We have added some belief ratings, also incorporated into the in-session exposure procedures that may encourage more in-depth processing of the evidence for and against the automatic thoughts and rationale responses. Additionally, in the therapist manual, we have attempted to provide new therapists with a better sense of which cognitions are best to address at which point in therapy as well as a better understanding of the process by which experienced therapists not only help clients to challenge their original automatic thoughts but also help clients to challenge additional distorted thinking revealed during the cognitive restructuring process.

Throughout the manuals there is increased emphasis on the role of safety behaviors. Although this concept appeared in the previous edition as discussions of subtle avoidance strategies, the more explicit notion of safety behaviors that interfere with exposure and cognitive change reflects current scientific work in the area.

We have updated the session outlines that many people find helpful in conducting this treatment, especially for the first time. These appear on the Oxford University Press Web site at www.oup.com/us/ttw.

We are indebted to the numerous people who provided feedback over the years that lead to this revised edition. We have tried to distill that feedback into practical improvements. We hope that you will find this revised manual helpful as you work with socially anxious individuals.

Debra A. Hope
Richard G. Heimberg
Cynthia L. Turk

Acknowledgments

When writing this Therapist Guide our goal was to provide a useful companion to our client workbook, *Managing Social Anxiety: A Cognitive-Behavioral Approach*, and we hope that the material and the format will facilitate your work with socially anxious clients. In this second edition, we are pleased to be able to include our latest research findings and ongoing understanding of nature and treatment of social anxiety. Helping individuals overcome social anxiety is often challenging and, at times, frustrating. Mostly though, we have found it to be rewarding. We are happy to share what we have learned form our research and clinical experience with other therapists.

We would like to thank the numerous people who have contributed to the development of this volume. Many individuals seeking treatment for social anxiety have helped us in our research by sharing their lives and struggles with us. We are grateful for their trust. It is a privilege to be the conduit by which their research participation helps alleviate the suffering of others who also struggle with social anxiety. The many doctoral students and postdoctoral fellows who served as therapists have improved this manual by providing their own insights into the treatment procedures. Although they are too numerous to name individually, we appreciate their contributions. We have also been fortunate to benefit from many therapists who have been using the first edition of this manual and client workbook around the world and give us informal feedback about what they find helpful. Brandon Weiss and Jodi Wiser provided excellent assistance with the manuscript and some of the figures. We are grateful to Mariclaire Cloutier who helped bring this manual under the Treatments *ThatWork*™ umbrella when she was at Oxford University Press. Our appreciation to Joan Bossert and Cristina Wojdylo at Oxford University Press for helping to bring this revision to fruition. Finally, we would like to thank our colleagues whose ideas have influenced our own thinking over the years. In particular, we are grateful to Aaron T. Beck, MD, Jacqueline Persons, PhD, and Edna Foa, PhD. David Barlow, PhD, has patiently encouraged this project and we appreciate his support.

Contents

Background for Therapists

Chapter 1 | *Introduction and Treatment Considerations*

The second edition of *Managing Social Anxiety: A Cognitive-Behavioral Therapy Approach—Client Workbook* and this companion Therapist Guide present a great deal of information on the nature of social anxiety, the cognitive-behavioral techniques used to treat it, how to best implement these techniques, and how to deal with the problems that arise during treatment. We hope that making this package available to clinicians will serve to more widely disseminate this empirically supported therapy, further stimulate research on the nature and treatment of social anxiety, and ultimately improve the lives of individuals suffering its disruptive effects. The second edition builds upon the original work but also includes much that we have learned since its publication in 2000. We hope that these volumes will be shown to build on our earlier successes as well as to benefit from our earlier mistakes.

Clinicians using this treatment program should first read the client workbook, because the therapist guide was written with the assumption that the reader is familiar with its contents. After reading the client workbook, most clinicians should be able to rely exclusively on the therapist guide to conduct treatment sessions. For therapists less familiar with this treatment approach, detailed session outlines are available at www.oup.com/us/ttw. These outlines are very helpful in guiding the sessions for therapists new to this treatment. The early chapters of this therapist guide address how we envision the implementation of this treatment, provide additional background information on social anxiety and its treatment, and describe our recommendations for pretreatment, ongoing, and posttreatment assessment. The middle chapters present summaries of each chapter in the client workbook for easy reference and provide pointers for communicating key concepts and relating those concepts to the client's experience. Later chapters focus primarily on how to conduct effective exposures, including ideas for exposures and recommendations for troubleshooting commonly occurring problems.

Treatment Modality

The client workbook was developed with the expectation that it would be used most frequently for individual treatment. Nevertheless, we envision a variety of additional uses including as an adjunct to group treatment, for combined group and individual treatment, for self-help, as a client-directed supplement to pharmacotherapy, and as adjunctive treatment for other problems such as marital discord or substance abuse when social anxiety seems to be contributing to the problem.

The vast majority of research studies supporting the efficacy of cognitive restructuring and exposure have applied these interventions under the supervision of a therapist. Little is known about the efficacy of these procedures with little or no therapist guidance (e.g., self-help, client-directed supplement to another treatment). We encourage research that helps us better specify the optimal level of clinician involvement for different groups of individuals experiencing problematic social anxiety.

Although multiple studies have demonstrated the efficacy of cognitive restructuring and exposure under the supervision of a therapist, very little research is available to address the question of whether these techniques are best delivered in the context of a group, individual treatment, or some combination of group and individual treatment. Several meta-analyses of the cognitive-behavioral treatment of social anxiety disorder suggest that group and individual treatment are associated with similar effect sizes (e.g., Acarturk, Cuijpers, van Straten, & de Graaf, 2009; Fedoroff & Taylor, 2001; Gould, Buckminster, Pollack, Otto, & Yap, 1997; Powers, Sigmarsson, & Emmelkamp, 2008; Taylor, 1996), and only one empirical study suggests that there is a difference, slightly favoring individual treatment (Stangier, Heidenreich, Peitz, Lauterbach, & Clark, 2003). Given the lack of research on this issue, we present what we see as the advantages and disadvantages of conducting this treatment in group and individual modalities. For a detailed presentation of our treatment approach tailored to a group format, see Heimberg and Becker (2002).

A group format provides a number of advantages. Social anxiety can sometimes lead to extreme isolation. Affected persons may feel ashamed of their fears, and many have never discussed them with another person. The therapy group has great power to normalize the experience of social anxiety by facilitating contact with others who have similar thoughts and feelings. Within a group, clients are able to support and encourage each other's efforts and commitment to change and learn from each other's attempts to overcome their fears. A group also facilitates in-session exposures because group members are readily available to serve as role play partners or audience members. Furthermore, group members assist in challenging an individual's distorted thinking during cognitive restructuring and can provide feedback on the quality of an individual's performance during an exposure. In many cases, input from group members is more powerful and credible than is feedback presented by an individual therapist.

One of the greatest disadvantages of the group format is that obtaining an adequate number of appropriate clients can be challenging—if not impossible—in many clinical settings. Furthermore, not all clients with social anxiety disorder are well suited for participation in a group. Clients who are excessively hostile, who are demanding of attention, or who exhibit severe personality pathology are likely to interfere with the group process and detract from the quality of treatment received by the other members. On rare occasions, a client will present with such severe social anxiety that he will have difficulty concentrating and learning the concepts presented in the group. Such an individual may attempt to reduce his anxiety by not participating in sessions or by avoiding sessions. These clients are best served, at least initially, in individual treatment.

Individual treatment provides greater flexibility in terms of the pace and duration of therapy and the extent to which issues in addition to social anxiety can be addressed if needed. Clients are also able to spend more time with a therapist addressing their idiosyncratic maladaptive beliefs and are not required to spend time observing others struggling with distorted thoughts and participating in exposures that may not be directly relevant to their personal concerns.

Probably the greatest disadvantage of individual treatment is that, in many clinical settings, it is difficult to have a variety of role play partners on hand for exposures and the therapist must act as a role player more often than in group treatment. It may be challenging for the therapist to both participate and observe the client's behavior during in-session exposures (i.e., simultaneously monitoring the client's anxiety level, tracking whether the client is meeting his goals, timing the exposure, and participating in the social task at hand). Furthermore, the client's familiarity with the therapist may sometimes prevent adequate levels of anxiety from being aroused, which may interfere with habituation of anxiety during exposures (Hayes, Hope, VanDyke, & Heimberg, 2007). Later chapters in this therapist guide provide suggestions for dealing with these and other issues related to conducting effective exposures.

Therapists

In our research program, psychologists and doctoral students in clinical or counseling psychology with a background in cognitive-behavioral therapy have served as therapists. The ideal therapist conducting this treatment is intimately familiar with cognitive-behavioral theory, has an understanding of social anxiety from a cognitive-behavioral perspective, and possesses good basic therapeutic skills. One of our goals with this program, however, is to more widely disseminate this treatment. We hope that the client workbook and the therapist guide are sufficiently detailed to allow relatively new therapists and therapists from different theoretical orientations and professional disciplines to provide this treatment. Such therapists would mostly likely benefit from supervision and consultation with an experienced cognitive-behavioral therapist on their first few cases and the more complex cases they encounter.

When conducting group treatment, sessions are best led by two cotherapists. Although we have conducted single-therapist groups on occasion, this approach is typically quite challenging and fatiguing for the therapist. Groups are also best served by one therapist of each gender. This arrangement allows for the greatest flexibility in creating relevant in-session exposures because many clients fear interactions with the opposite sex. Furthermore, clients who present with extreme fears of interaction with the opposite sex may be afraid to interact with a therapist of the opposite sex and may find the group much less threatening if there is a same-sex therapist available.

Concomitant Medications

Many clients will be taking one or more psychotropic medications when they present for treatment. Some will be taking the medication with the specific intention of managing their social anxiety. Several different medications have been shown to be efficacious in the treatment of social anxiety disorder (See for reviews Blackmore, Erwin, Heimberg, Magee, & Fresco, 2009; and Schneier, Erwin, Heimberg, Marshall, & Mellman, 2007). Of course, we rarely see the client whose medication use has been associated with the remission of their anxiety—there is just no incentive for that person to seek cognitive-behavioral treatment. Unfortunately, however, we have found that many clients are taking medications that lack empirical support for their efficacy for social anxiety disorder (or for which research suggests lack of efficacy) or are taking a dosage of a potentially appropriate medication that is below the recommended range.

Furthermore, our clinical experience suggests that many clients have a minimal understanding of how their medication works, other available medication options, the possible impact of these drugs on cognitive-behavioral therapy, and so on. If the therapist is not the prescribing physician, he or she should establish a collaborative relationship with the prescribing physician as soon as possible and come to an agreement about the best way to coordinate therapy and pharmacological treatment. Changing dosages of an existing medication, switching to or adding another medication, discontinuing an existing medication, or tapering medication over the course of therapy are all options that may be appropriate for different clients.

When it is not required for enrollment in a randomized controlled trial, we do not believe that it is necessary for clients to discontinue their medications prior to starting this program. In fact, we recommend helping clients already taking medications to evaluate and, if needed or desired, work in consultation with their physicians to modify or discontinue their current regimen. We do discourage clients from repeatedly adjusting their medication regimen during the course of therapy because, clinically, we want them to be able to attribute positive changes in their symptoms to their own efforts as much as possible. For individuals who take medication on an "as needed" basis, we do ask that they refrain from taking it before therapy sessions or exposure homework assignments.

For currently unmedicated clients, in the majority of cases, we would recommend a trial of this program before pursuing medication options. Exceptions may include clients who are so socially anxious that they have difficulty tolerating the interpersonal demands of therapy or who desire rapid symptom reduction because they are facing an acute social stressor (e.g., starting a new job with significant social demands).

Chapter 2   *Supplemental Information on Social Anxiety*

The goal of this chapter is to provide the therapist with background information on social anxiety and its treatment beyond that provided in the client workbook. We begin this chapter with a brief overview of the epidemiology and psychopathology of social anxiety disorder. We then present our model of social anxiety in greater detail than in the client workbook to more thoroughly introduce the theoretical underpinnings of our treatment.

Epidemiology and Psychopathology

In the National Comorbidity Survey Replication (NCS-R), 9282 non-institutionalized individuals 18 years of age and older throughout the United States were interviewed about various mental health problems. This study found that 12.1% of people suffer from clinically significant social anxiety at some point during their lives (Kessler et al., 2005). In fact, social anxiety disorder was the fourth most common psychiatric disorder, with only major depressive disorder, alcohol abuse, and specific phobia having a higher lifetime prevalence rate. When the investigators examined social anxiety disorder during the past year, the prevalence rate was 6.8%, second only to specific phobia (Kessler, Chiu, Demler, Merikangas, & Walters, 2005). Social anxiety most commonly begins during early childhood or adolescence (Schneier, Johnson, Hornig, Liebowitz, & Weissman, 1992) and typically follows a chronic and unremitting course (Chartier, Hazen, & Stein, 1998; Reich, Goldenberg, Vasile, Goisman, & Keller, 1994).

Unfortunately, most individuals with social anxiety disorder do not seek treatment unless they develop an additional disorder (Schneier et al.,

1992). Approximately 70% to 80% of individuals with social anxiety disorder meet criteria for additional diagnoses (Magee, Eaton, Wittchen, McGonagle, & Kessler, 1996; Schneier et al., 1992), and the percentage of comorbid cases increases among persons who endorse a larger number of feared social situations (Ruscio et al., 2008). In most cases, the onset of social anxiety disorder predates the onset of these comorbid conditions. In community samples, the most common additional diagnoses include specific phobia, agoraphobia, major depression, and alcohol abuse and dependence (Magee et al., 1996; Schneier et al., 1992). Among treatment-seeking clients, comorbidity with depression is associated with more severe impairment before and after cognitive-behavioral treatment (e.g., Erwin, Heimberg, Juster, & Mindlin, 2002). However, individuals with and without comorbid conditions make similar gains. These findings suggest that socially anxious individuals with comorbid mood disorders may benefit from more extended treatment for their social anxiety or supplemental treatment directed at the comorbid disorder. Comorbid mood disorders appear to be more strongly associated with greater pretreatment and posttreatment impairment than comorbid anxiety disorders (Erwin et al., 2002).

Subtypes of Social Anxiety Disorder and Avoidant Personality Disorder

Both clinical experience and research suggest that individuals presenting for treatment of social anxiety are a heterogeneous group in terms of pervasiveness and severity of their social fears. In the current diagnostic system, the *generalized* subtype of social anxiety disorder is specified if most social situations are feared. Social interaction fears (e.g., dating, joining an ongoing conversation, being assertive), performance fears (e.g., public speaking, playing a musical instrument in front of others), and observation fears (e.g., working in front of others, walking down the street) are common among these clients.

The *Diagnostic and Statistical Manual of Mental Disorders, fourth edition* (DSM-IV) also classifies clients with limited fears into the *nongeneralized* subtype of social anxiety disorder, "a heterogeneous group that includes persons who fear a single performance situation as well as those who fear several, but not most, social situations" (American Psychiatric

Association [APA], 1994, p. 413). For example, clients who fear public speaking but otherwise feel comfortable interacting with and being observed by others would be assigned to the nongeneralized subtype.

Clients with generalized social anxiety disorder improve as much as nongeneralized clients do with cognitive-behavioral treatment (Brown, Heimberg, & Juster, 1995; Hope, Herbert, & White, 1995; Turner, Beidel, Wolff, Spaulding, & Jacob, 1996). However, because clients with generalized social anxiety disorder begin treatment with greater impairment, they remain more impaired after receiving the same number of treatment sessions. These findings suggest that clients with generalized social anxiety may require a longer course of treatment to achieve outcomes similar to those of clients with nongeneralized social anxiety.

The generalized subtype of social anxiety disorder has many features in common with avoidant personality disorder (APD). In the current diagnostic system, APD is characterized by a long-standing pattern "of social inhibition, feelings of inadequacy, and hypersensitivity to negative evaluation..." (APA, 1994, p. 664). Given the similarity between the descriptions of the two disorders, it is not surprising that many clients who meet diagnostic criteria for social anxiety disorder also meet criteria for APD. However, there is little scientific evidence to suggest that some individuals meet criteria for APD without also meeting criteria for social anxiety disorder (Widiger, 1992). The most parsimonious description of the relationship between social anxiety disorder and APD is that they are not different disorders and that individuals meeting criteria for both disorders are simply the most severely impaired persons with social anxiety disorder (Heimberg, Holt, Schneier, Spitzer, & Liebowitz, 1993). With regard to treatment outcome, some studies have found that clients with and without comorbid APD make similar gains (Brown et al., 1995; Hofmann, Newman, Becker, Taylor, & Roth, 1995; Hope, Herbert, et al., 1995), although others have found comorbid APD to be associated with a poorer treatment response (Chambless, Tran, & Glass, 1997; Feske, Perry, Chambless, Renneberg, & Goldstein, 1996). Nevertheless, the effects of APD on treatment have been smaller than anticipated, and a substantial number of clients no longer met criteria for APD following 12 weeks of cognitive-behavioral treatment for social anxiety (Brown et al., 1995). The remediation of APD within such a brief time frame further calls into question the conceptualization of this symptom cluster as representing a distinct personality disorder. As with individuals meeting criteria for generalized social anxiety disorder, clients with APD may require a longer course of treatment to achieve an optimal outcome.

The notion of subtyping socially anxious individuals is not without controversy. This system basically takes a dimensional variable (i.e., number of social situations feared) and turns it into a categorical variable (i.e., generalized versus nongeneralized subtypes). Although it is clear that there are some qualitative differences between the subtypes (e.g., the generalized subtype appears to run in families, whereas the nongeneralized subtype does not; Stein et al., 1998), there is also evidence to suggest that simply counting the number of feared social situations a person endorses may provide as much information as the current subtyping scheme (Vriends, Becker, Meyer, Michael, & Margraf, 2007). The degree of impairment demonstrated by persons with social anxiety disorder in the NCS-R was directly related to the number of social situations feared (Ruscio et al., 2008).

Beliefs

Through a complex interaction of genetics, family environment, and important life experiences, socially anxious individuals develop fundamental, negative beliefs about themselves, others, and the social world. One common belief among socially anxious individuals is that they lack important social skills and that their social behavior is likely to be inadequate or inappropriate. Research has repeatedly demonstrated that socially anxious individuals are more critical of their own social behavior than are objective observers (Norton & Hope, 2001; Rapee & Lim, 1992; Stopa & Clark, 1993). Therefore, many socially anxious individuals may give a description of their social behavior that is more reflective of their negative beliefs than of their actual performance. Although some research has suggested that socially anxious individuals exhibit deficient social behavior (Halford & Foddy, 1982; Stopa & Clark, 1993), other research suggests that their social behavior is satisfactory (Glasgow & Arkowitz, 1975; Rapee & Lim, 1992).

We believe that it is important to clarify the difference between "performance deficits" and "social skills deficits." We believe that the term *social skills deficit* should be applied only when a person cannot perform the behavior in question or cannot perform it up to a certain standard because she does not know how. Therefore, even when performance deficits are observed among socially anxious individuals, it is difficult, if not impossible, to tease apart whether these deficiencies are a function of a lack of social knowledge, of behavioral inhibition produced by anxiety, or of some combination of these and other factors. Nevertheless, we have observed that the behavior of most socially anxious individuals during in-session exposures is within the normal range and that social behavior improves as anxiety declines. This may happen for several reasons. For example, a reduction of negative thoughts through cognitive restructuring may improve an individual's ability to attend to the social task at hand and improve performance. Eliminating subtle avoidance behaviors such as poor eye contact through exposures may also have a positive impact upon performance. In fact, research has shown that exposure and cognitive restructuring alone (i.e., with no explicit social skills training) has a positive impact upon the quality of social behavior according to the ratings of objective observers (e.g., Heimberg, Salzman, Holt, & Blendell, 1993; Hope, Heimberg, & Bruch, 1995). Thus, our approach is to work from the assumption that, in most cases, performance deficits may be remedied by exposure and cognitive restructuring and do not require explicit training in social skills. Of course, when assessment of a specific client suggests otherwise, social skills training can easily be added to our program, and at least one study suggests that this may be a beneficial strategy (Herbert et al., 2005).

Another set of commonly held beliefs among socially anxious individuals is that they will display noticeable anxiety symptoms (e.g., blushing, trembling, or sweating) and that others will interpret these symptoms as reflecting mental illness or other negative characteristics (Roth, Antony, & Swinson, 2001). In contrast, nonanxious persons are more likely to think that others would judge these symptoms to reflect a normal physical state such as being cold, tired, or hungry. Although socially anxious individuals have been shown to display more symptoms of anxiety than their nonanxious counterparts, they routinely overestimate the visibility of their anxiety symptoms relative to ratings by objective observers (Alden & Wallace, 1995; Bruch, Gorsky, Collins, & Berger, 1989; McEwan & Devins, 1983).

Socially anxious individuals may also believe that social relationships are inherently competitive and hierarchical in nature (Gilbert, 2001; Trower & Gilbert, 1989; Walters & Hope, 1998). Socially anxious persons often doubt that they will be able to successfully compete for dominant positions in the social hierarchy. Thus, instead of making dominance a primary goal during interactions, they may adopt secondary goals such as remaining affiliated with the group, retaining current social status, and avoiding harm. These goals require that they remain hypervigilant so that they can quickly detect signals of threat from others and that they behave in a manner that communicates a subordinate position to others perceived as dominant. If these strategies for remaining affiliated with others are perceived as failing, escape and avoidance behaviors are likely. In contrast, nonanxious individuals tend to view social relationships as cooperative and supportive most of the time. For example, a socially anxious individual may view a conversation with a new coworker as some sort of competition in which each person looks for weaknesses in the other (e.g., who is more attractive, well educated) and as a potential threat to her status and self-esteem. A nonanxious person would be more likely to view the same conversation as an opportunity to pleasantly pass the time, make a new friend, get input on a project, and so forth.

Information Processing

Research has shown that socially anxious persons exhibit biases in the allocation of attention that favor the detection of social threat cues in the environment (e.g., Asmundson & Stein, 1994; Hope, Rapee, Heimberg, & Dombeck, 1990; Mattia, Heimberg, & Hope, 1993; Sposari & Rapee, 2007; see reviews by Hirsch & Clark, 2004, and Schultz & Heimberg, 2008), a phenomenon referred to as "wearing amber-colored glasses" in the client workbook. In a study by Veljaca and Rapee (1998), socially anxious participants detected significantly more negative than positive reactions from audience members during a presentation, suggesting an attentional bias for threatening social information. In contrast, nonanxious participants detected significantly more positive than negative reactions, suggesting that they were biased toward detecting social cues indicative of safety and acceptance.

Such biased attention holds the potential for several negative consequences. A bias for negative social information may interfere with the socially anxious individual's ability to process information contrary to existing beliefs. Therefore, the audience member who yawns is attended to and the other audience members who may be smiling or nodding are largely ignored. A negative attentional bias may also magnify the importance of social information interpreted as threatening, such that one's perception that her voice is trembling is equated with weakness of character and not knowing the answer to a question is taken as a reflection of one's incompetence (a point of view that is known as the combined cognitive bias hypothesis; Hirsch, Clark, & Mathews, 2006). Lastly, hypervigilance for social threat may drain cognitive resources and interfere with the individual's ability to attend and respond appropriately to the social task at hand. For example, one may lose one's place during a speech or have difficulty responding to questions during a conversation.

Post-Event Processing

A growing literature suggests the importance of post-event processing in the maintenance of social anxiety disorder (see review by Brozovich & Heimberg, 2008). First described by Clark and Wells (1995), post-event processing may be defined as the person's detailed review of her performance following a social situation. Although this may not be problematic for everyone and may be beneficial for some, the attentional and interpretive biases of persons with social anxiety disorder increase the chances that post-event processing will lead to a reconstruction of the memory of the situation so that it is recalled as more negative than originally perceived. In fact, a number of studies have demonstrated a relationship between post-event processing and increasingly negative recall over time of one's performance in social interaction or public speaking tasks (Abbott & Rapee, 2004; Dannahy & Stopa,

2007; Edwards, Rapee, & Franklin, 2003; Perini, Abbott, & Rapee, 2006). The negative effects on the socially anxious person's belief in her ability to successfully confront the situation the next time it occurs are potentially great and underscore the need for cognitive restructuring activities after in-session and *in vivo* exposure assignments.

An Integrated Cognitive-Behavioral Model of Social Anxiety Disorder

We now present the model of social anxiety that provides the conceptual framework for the procedures used in our treatment (Heimberg & Becker, 2002; Rapee & Heimberg, 1997; Roth & Heimberg, 2001; Turk, Lerner, Heimberg, & Rapee, 2001). Our model focuses on how social anxiety is maintained rather than on how it develops (see chapter 4 of the client workbook for a discussion of etiology). Specifically, it portrays what happens when socially anxious individuals face a situation that they perceive as holding the potential for negative evaluation.

The cognitive-behavioral model presented here is more sophisticated than is the more generic model presented to clients (see chapter 2 of the client workbook). We believe that an understanding of the more complex model can facilitate case conceptualization for therapists. However, we believe that the scaled-down model presented in the client workbook is sufficient to help clients begin to reconceptualize their social anxiety and understand the rationale behind treatment. Little benefit will be derived from overwhelming already anxious clients with too much detail.

Figure 2.1 illustrates what takes place when a socially anxious individual confronts a social situation that she perceives as holding the potential for negative evaluation. When confronted with another person or persons (i.e., "the audience"), she forms a mental image of how she appears to the audience. This mental image is formed using information from long-term memory, current internal cues such as one's face feeling hot, and external cues such as the other person's gestures or facial expressions. These images may include spontaneous, recurrent images of events that occurred around the time of the onset of the disorder (Hackmann, Clark, & McManus, 2000). Socially anxious persons are more likely to form images and memories of threatening

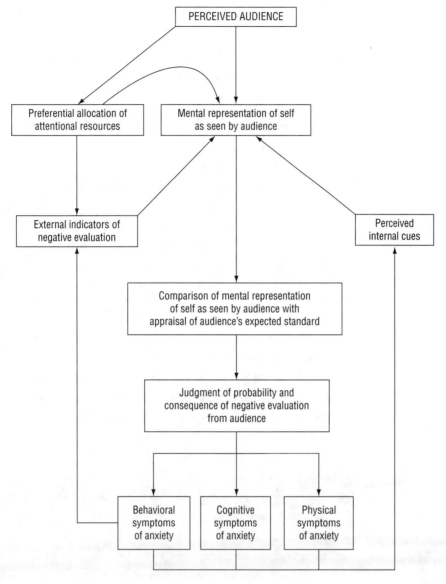

Figure 2.1

A Model of the Generation and Maintenance of Anxiety in Social/Evaluative Situations.

From Rapee, R. M. & Heimberg R. C. (1997). A cognitive-behavioral model of anxiety in social phobia. *Behaviour Research and Therapy, 35,* 743. Copyright © 1997 by Elsevier Science. Reprinted by permission. All rights reserved.

social situations in which they see themselves from an external point of view (e.g., Hackmann, Surawy, & Clark, 1998; Wells, Clark, & Ahmad, 1998). This phenomenon is not surprising in that socially anxious individuals are most concerned with how they appear to others and whether anything in their appearance might elicit a negative reaction. In contrast, nonanxious individuals are more likely to remember threatening social situations from a field perspective, in which they recall people and things in the environment as seen through their own eyes (e.g., Coles, Turk, Heimberg, & Fresco, 2001).

The mental representation of the self as seen by others is likely to be distorted in a manner consistent with the individual's negative beliefs about her behavior and appearance. For example, a recent client with a slight Australian accent described his speech as "muttering," "mumbling," and "hard to understand." Role players during his in-session exposures described him as "charming," "pleasant," and "not at all difficult to understand." Another client became tearful and described herself as "ugly" and "unacceptable," because she perceived her jaw line as protruding grossly from her face, despite the fact that this feature objectively appeared to be well within the normal range.

During the social encounter, the socially anxious individual constantly monitors and adjusts the mental representation of the self on the basis of internal and external cues. For example, a socially anxious person giving a lecture would be likely to detect the slightest hand tremor when writing on the blackboard and would then include (and probably exaggerate) this information in the mental image of the self. As previously noted, this individual would also preferentially allocate attentional resources to quickly detect feedback suggestive of negative evaluation from the audience (e.g., frowns). Therefore, the person attempts to simultaneously monitor her appearance and behavior for anything unacceptable, monitor the environment for evidence of negative evaluation, *and* engage in the ongoing social task. This division of attentional resources *may* disrupt social performance, which *may* elicit actual negative feedback from others (which in turn would provoke a downward adjustment of the mental representation of the self as seen by others and an increase in anxiety symptoms). Complex social tasks, which require more processing resources, may be more likely to result in disrupted performance than simpler ones.

The socially anxious individual takes her (distorted) mental self-representation and compares it with what she perceives to be the standard held by the audience. Characteristics of the audience (e.g., education level, attractiveness) and features of the situation (e.g., whether it is a brief or extended social task, whether the situation is structured or unstructured) influence how lofty the audience's standards are judged to be. Given the negative bias present in the mental self-representation, in many instances, the individual will judge herself as falling short of the audience's expectations. In the instances in which the individual perceives herself as appearing and behaving in a manner consistent with or exceeding the estimated standards of the audience, anxiety will be minimal. For example, an individual may feel relatively comfortable giving weekly reports to subordinates but extremely anxious giving the same report to a supervisor, who may be perceived as holding higher standards for performance. Lastly, predictions that the likelihood of negative evaluation is high and the consequences of negative evaluation are catastrophic lead to cognitive, behavioral, and physiological symptoms of anxiety. These cognitive, behavioral, and physiological symptoms interact with each other and eventually feed back into and further bias the mental representation of the self, perpetuating the cycle of anxiety.

The model suggests several points of intervention in the treatment of social anxiety disorder. It also highlights several aspects of the disorder that should be addressed in the treatment. These include (Heimberg & Becker, 2002):

- Negative beliefs about social situations and other people

- Negative beliefs about oneself

- Negative predictions about the outcomes of social situations

- Avoidance associated with these negative predictions

- Attentional focus on social threat cues while engaged in the social situation

- Negative evaluation of performance after the situation has passed

Our treatment works to break the vicious cycle of anxiety described in the model through the use of cognitive interventions before, during, and after in-session and *in vivo* exposures. Chapter 2 of the client workbook provides a rationale for the use of cognitive restructuring and exposure as well as the importance of in-session exposures and homework.

Chapter 3 | *Assessment of Social Anxiety Disorder*

Assessment and therapy are inexorably intertwined in our treatment approach. This chapter focuses on what we perceive as being an adequate pretreatment assessment and addresses the role of assessment throughout treatment. Readers seeking a more thorough review of assessment and psychometric issues are referred to Hart, Jack, Turk, and Heimberg (1999) and Heimberg and Turk (2002).

Pretreatment Assessment

Assessing for Clinically Significant Social Anxiety

In most clinical settings, the client's first session consists of an unstructured clinical interview. As discussed in chapter 2 of this therapist guide, because individuals with social anxiety disorder do not typically seek treatment unless they have a comorbid diagnosis, and because healthcare professionals often fail to detect clinically significant social anxiety, we recommend that all intake interviews routinely include questions screening for problems with social anxiety. Research has revealed that clients obtaining a total score of 6 or more on three statements derived from the Social Phobia Inventory (SPIN; Connor et al., 2000) are likely to meet diagnostic criteria for social anxiety disorder (Connor, Kobak, Churchill, Katzelnick, & Davidson, 2001; Katzelnick et al., 2001). These items, referred to as the "Mini-SPIN," are "Fear of embarrassment causes me to avoid doing things or speaking to people," "I avoid activities in which I am the center of attention," and "Being embarrassed or looking stupid are among my worst fears." Each item is rated on a 5-point scale as follows: 0 = not at all; 1 = a little bit; 2 = somewhat;

3 = very much; 4 = extremely. At the Adult Anxiety Clinic of Temple, we have used the Mini-SPIN as a brief telephone screening instrument for some time, and it has proven to have substantial utility. Furthermore, among callers who later came to the clinic for evaluation, the Mini-SPIN was significantly correlated with other measures of social anxiety and functional disability, but not with measures of generalized anxiety/worry, depression, or anxiety sensitivity (Weeks, Spokas, & Heimberg, 2007).

We present the Mini-SPIN as one method that may be used to initially screen for the presence of clinically significant social anxiety. Naturally, once the clinician suspects that social anxiety is a problem for any given client, a more thorough assessment is necessary to arrive at a diagnosis of social anxiety disorder according to DSM-IV criteria. The clinician-administered and self-report instruments described in this chapter can be helpful in clarifying whether the social anxiety is within the normal range or suggestive of clinically significant difficulties. Semi-structured clinical interviews can also be helpful in terms of detecting social anxiety disorder as well as assisting with differential diagnosis and assessing comorbid conditions that may affect the course of treatment. Commonly used semi-structured clinical interviews include the Anxiety Disorders Interview Schedule for DSM-IV: Lifetime Version (ADIS-IV-L; DiNardo, Brown, & Barlow, 1994), and the Structured Clinical Interview for DSM-IV-TR Axis I disorders—Patient Edition (SCID-I/P; First, Spitzer, Gibbon, & Williams, 2002). Although in many settings unstructured interviews are favored over semi-structured interviews due to financial, time, and training constraints, we recommend having copies of one or more of these interviews on hand for use with clients with particularly complex presentations.

Differential Diagnosis

At times it may be difficult to determine whether a client's symptoms are best characterized as features of social anxiety disorder or some other disorder. One of the more challenging differential diagnostic decisions can be between social anxiety disorder and panic disorder. Individuals with social anxiety disorder may occasionally or routinely experience panic attacks in social situations. Individuals with panic disorder may also experience panic attacks in social situations and feel embarrassed about how others may perceive them if they abruptly leave due to panicky feelings or if their anxiety symptoms are noticeable. Despite these overlapping features, these disorders can be distinguished. Making the correct diagnosis is important because different approaches to treatment may be indicated.

One question to consider is whether the individual is primarily afraid of the symptoms themselves or that the symptoms will lead to negative evaluation. Individuals with panic disorder would be expected to be concerned about the anxiety symptoms even if they were alone and no one witnessed their panic attack. Individuals with social anxiety disorder, in contrast, would be expected to be most concerned that others will see their anxiety symptoms and evaluate them negatively on that basis.

Another question to consider is whether panic attacks occur in nonsocial situations or, conversely, whether panic attacks occur exclusively in certain social situations. A diagnosis of panic disorder with agoraphobia is more likely to be warranted if the individual is afraid of having a panic attack in at least some situations in which social evaluation is unlikely (e.g., when alone, during sleep, going over a bridge). Additionally, social anxiety disorder should be considered if the panic attacks occur exclusively during or when anticipating a feared social situation (e.g., giving a speech). Importantly, social anxiety disorder and panic disorder can co-occur, and some individuals meet criteria for both disorders. In these cases, an agreement should be reached between the client and the clinician regarding which disorder should be the initial focus of treatment.

We are occasionally asked how to differentiate social anxiety disorder from paranoid personality disorder or "paranoia" in general. It is true that some socially anxious clients report social-evaluative concerns that seem quite improbable to people without the disorder. For example, it may seem "paranoid" for socially anxious clients to fear that they are being laughed at by strangers in restaurants, being criticized by people walking down the street, or being otherwise scrutinized by strangers in what are innocuous situations for most people. This hypervigilance to negative evaluation may seem "paranoid" to most people who do not view others as sources of painful rejection or who do not view themselves as fundamentally unacceptable to others. Such reports from socially anxious clients, especially ones with more generalized fears, are not uncommon and can be conceptualized as part of the presentation of social anxiety disorder rather than as an alternative or additional diagnosis. Furthermore, in most cases, there is at least some recognition that these types of fears are either excessive or unreasonable. Clients meeting criteria for paranoid personality disorder would be expected, in contrast, to have less concern about falling short of the standards of others. Instead, they would be more likely to view their own behavior as reasonable and the behavior of others as unjustifiably malevolent.

We have also been asked to distinguish between severe social anxiety disorder and schizoid personality disorder. Schizoid individuals do not desire or enjoy close relationships. Socially anxious persons, in contrast, yearn for the social contact they fear. Occasionally, persons with social anxiety disorder will, during the course of treatment, make statements such as "Maybe I am just not interested in making conversation with coworkers" or "I don't care about dating"—even when these statements could not be further from the truth. In most instances, gentle probing will reveal that these statements are reflective of intense anxiety regarding confronting a feared social situation and the associated desire to avoid it, as opposed to a genuine lack of interest in other people.

Importance of the Diagnostic Evaluation

The time devoted to a thorough diagnostic evaluation is time well spent. Clients whose symptoms are better accounted for by a diagnosis other than social anxiety disorder may experience little improvement with this treatment and may experience, among other things, increased frustration, hopelessness, and financial hardship. In instances when misdiagnosed clients are included in a group treatment, the group process is likely to be disrupted as the client's poor fit with the group becomes apparent.

A thorough diagnostic assessment is also important in determining whether social anxiety disorder is only one aspect of a more complex clinical picture. As discussed in chapter 2 of this therapist guide, comorbidity is common among persons with social anxiety disorder. We routinely treat clients with comorbid anxiety and mood disorders in both group and individual treatment. As noted earlier, that comorbidity is associated with greater pretreatment and posttreatment impairment, but it does not preclude significant therapeutic benefit. Comorbidity should suggest to the therapist and the client that more extended treatment of social anxiety or supplemental treatment directed at the comorbid disorder may be required for the client to achieve optimal end-state functioning.

For clients highly impaired by disorders or life problems in addition to social anxiety, the clinician and the client should come to an agreement regarding what the initial focus of treatment should be. Severe depression, substance dependence, uncontrolled bipolar disorder, severe eating disorders, or acute life stressors (e.g., bereavement) would be examples of problems that, in most cases, would need to be addressed prior to initiating this treatment program. In the case of individual therapy, treatments can be sequenced or integrated in a manner that best meets the needs of the client.

Pretreatment Measures

The therapist should give the client feedback regarding the diagnoses arrived at (or being considered) following the initial interview. The therapist should also discuss the importance of completing additional assessments to understand more fully the nature of the client's social anxiety prior to starting treatment. We believe that an adequate pretreatment assessment battery consists of, at a minimum, self-report and clinician-rated measures of social anxiety and a behavior test, in which the client confronts one or more fear-provoking social situations within the clinic setting (see more on the use of behavior tests in clinical practice below). It should be possible to complete this battery over the course of one or two sessions.

Even for cases in which social anxiety is the presenting complaint and obviously the primary problem, administration of validated self-report and clinician-rated instruments is important. In the context of an initial clinical interview, shame and evaluative fears can lead clients to give descriptions of their problems that do not fully reflect the severity or pervasiveness of their social fear and avoidance. Administration of psychometrically sound self-report and clinician-rated measures facilitates the assessment of fear and avoidance in a broad range of social situations within a relatively brief time frame. Furthermore, the availability of data regarding the typical performance of socially anxious clients and normal controls allows the clinician to objectively evaluate the severity of a particular client's symptoms relative to meaningful reference points. Lastly, pretreatment scores provide a baseline against which progress can be objectively assessed.

Recommended Assessment Battery

To facilitate the pretreatment assessment, we have included copies of widely used measures of social anxiety, scoring information, and normative data in the appendix. For more information on the measures presented, please see Hart et al. (1999) and Heimberg and Turk (2002). In a standard pretreatment assessment battery we typically include the Social Interaction Anxiety Scale (SIAS) and Social Phobia Scale (SPS). These self-report instruments assess fear of interpersonal situations and fear of being scrutinized by others, respectively (Mattick & Clarke, 1998) and both have been shown to discriminate between persons with social anxiety disorder and those with other anxiety disorders (Brown et al., 1997; Heimberg, Mueller, Holt, Hope, & Liebowitz, 1992). To assess the fear of being judged unfavorably by others, we include the self-report Brief Fear of Negative Evaluation Scale (BFNE; Leary, 1983). Note that recent research suggests that for the BFNE (Rodebaugh et al., 2004; Weeks et al., 2005) and the SIAS (Rodebaugh, Woods, & Heimberg, 2007), the straightforwardly worded items may provide more valid measurement than those items that require reverse scoring; see the cited papers for details. However, we have included the standard BFNE and associated norms in the appendix. Finally, we administer the Liebowitz Social Anxiety Scale (LSAS; Liebowitz, 1987), which is a clinician-administered instrument designed to assess fear and avoidance of social interaction and performance situations. We have conducted considerable research on the psychometric characteristics of the LSAS and demonstrated that it is highly correlated with other measures of social anxiety, able to discriminate between persons with social anxiety disorder and persons with generalized anxiety disorder, and responsive to the effects of both cognitive-behavioral and pharmacological treatment (Fresco et al., 2001; Heimberg et al., 1998, 1999; Heimberg & Holaway, 2007; Mennin et al., 2002).

Additional Assessment Measures

Other instruments are available that were designed specifically for use in the assessment of social anxiety disorder. Probably the most commonly used self-report instrument not included in this manual is the Social Phobia and Anxiety Inventory (SPAI; Turner, Beidel, Dancu, & Stanley, 1989). The Brief Social Phobia Scale (BSPS; Davidson et al., 1991) is probably the next most frequently used clinician-administered instrument, following the LSAS.

A new self-report measure that may be worth serious consideration is the Subtle Avoidance Frequency Examination (SAFE), which measures the extent to which the client engages in a range of safety behaviors and other forms of subtle avoidance (Cuming et al., 2009). Three factors emerged from the SAFE, which appeared to reflect active safety behaviors, subtle restriction of behavior, and behaviors aimed at avoiding or concealing physical symptoms. The SAFE demonstrated strong internal consistency, good construct validity, and the ability to discriminate between clinical and nonclinical participants. In addition, the SAFE was responsive to the effects of treatment. Although further evaluation is required for this new measure, the SAFE may prove to be a useful measure both to identify avoidance behaviors that may be important to target in exposure-based treatment and to assess treatment outcome as an additional means.

Supplemental Assessment Measures

In addition to social anxiety instruments, we routinely administer measures that tap other constructs. We often administer the Beck Depression Inventory, 2nd edition (BDI-II), which assesses symptoms of depression (Beck, Steer, & Brown, 1996). Disability measures such as the Liebowitz Self-Rated Disability Scale (Schneier et al., 1994) are useful in assessing various levels of functional impairment across a number of domains. Perhaps the best standard by which to judge the impact of a treatment is its effect on the client's overall sense of well-being. Therefore, we also administer the Quality of Life Inventory, a self-report measure that assesses the extent to which clients perceive themselves as satisfied in the areas of their lives that they deem important to their happiness (Frisch, 1994).

Using Behavior Tests in Clinical Settings

Ideally, a behavior test is conducted prior to treatment. Behavior tests provide objective information about how anxious the client becomes during social interaction, performance, and/or observational situations. They also provide an objective index of the quality of the client's social behavior and help the therapist to estimate how likely the client's efforts are to be met with a positive response in the real world. This objective information cannot be replaced by self-report given that research has shown that socially anxious individuals describe their social behavior as more inadequate (e.g., Norton & Hope, 2001; Rapee & Lim, 1992; Stopa & Clark, 1993) and their anxiety as more obvious (e.g., Alden & Wallace, 1995) than do independent judges. A pretreatment behavior test can also provide valuable information that can be used to structure and calibrate the difficulty level of the first in-session exposure. As with self-report and clinician-administered measures, behavior tests can be readministered as a means of assessing reduction in anxiety and improvement in performance following treatment. Conducting behavioral tests can be challenging for therapists not familiar with them. Therapists who do not have behavioral training should consult a supplementary source before attempting a behavioral test. A detailed description of behavioral tests can be found in Heimberg and Becker (2002).

In our own clinical work, outside the research setting, we often use more informal procedures for behavioral tests than those used in research and described in Heimberg and Becker (2002). Typically the therapist will pick one or two situations from the client's feared situations that can be most easily staged in the treatment setting with just the therapist as a confederate. Most often the behavioral tests involve a conversation in a setting such as standing in line at a grocery store, assertiveness situation such as returning an unwanted item to a store, or giving a spontaneous talk to the therapist as the sole audience member. The therapist explains to the client that it is important for the therapist to see what these situations look like, and it is not usually feasible to go into real life situations with the client. The situation should be easy enough that the client will attempt it and, ideally, follow through for 3–4 min. The therapist can derive a great deal of information from the behavioral test including:

- Overall level of social skill and quality of performance

- Overall visibility of anxiety

- Visibility of specific anxiety symptoms that may be a focus of treatment such as a hand tremor

- Concordance between the client's self-report of social skill/quality of performance or visibility of anxiety symptoms and the impressions of the therapist, and

- Propensity of the client to avoid all or part of the situation or escape

The therapist can supplement this information by asking the client to report subjective anxiety levels before and after the experience as well as a retrospective peak anxiety during the role play. (It is not a good idea to interrupt the client for anxiety ratings, as is done during treatment, as this disrupts performance and is not necessary at this point.) Clients can also report the cognitions they experienced during the behavioral test. All of this information can serve as baseline data against which to measure change and guide case conceptualization regarding what cognitive biases may be primary for this particular individual. All of the measures listed above can be viewed qualitatively by the therapist or the therapist can easily think of them on a scale (e.g., 1–5 on social skills with 1 being inadequate performance, 5 being excellent performance). Making notes about the behavioral test and/or using a quantitative rating would allow the therapist to repeat the behavioral test later as a measure of client progress without the inevitable biases of memory.

We find behavioral tests extremely useful in case conceptualization and treatment planning. As noted previously, socially anxious individuals often believe they have deficient social skills. Most often this represents a biased perception of their own behavior or their anxiety is interfering with performance. However, occasionally true social skills deficits are an important part of the clinical picture. As described in Meier and Hope (1998), behavioral tests can help tease apart this difference. If a client can perform the requisite social skills during a behavior test, then the client's deficit is logically one in performance, not lack of skills. Therefore, if in the first behavioral test, the client demonstrates reasonable social skills, the assessment can stop, even if the client is convinced his skills are lacking. However, if performance is noticeably poor, then the therapist can conduct additional behavioral tests that evoke less anxiety. If the requisite skills are present in the less threatening behavioral test, then performance quality should improve when the client experiences less anxiety. As a last resort for highly anxious individuals, we often have the client give a verbal account of what one might say or how one might act in a given social situation. If, at a minimum, the client can state what skilled behavior would look like, then we proceed with the exposure-based treatment in this manual without additional skills training. However, if one cannot construct a behavioral test or elicit a verbal report that yields evidence of social skills, then the treatment plan should probably include some attention to the training of social skills.

When judging social skills or the visibility of anxiety symptoms, it is important for the therapist to consider the standards by which he or she is making that judgment. There are many very successful people who do not have perfect social skills. The standard of what is acceptable varies widely across cultures and situations. One does not have to have the oratory skills of Presidents John F. Kennedy, Ronald Reagan, or Barack Obama to make the report at a weekly staff meeting of 10 people. Verbal or nonverbal behaviors that will be viewed very negatively by many people or a clear lack of awareness of what is generally considered socially appropriate may require skills training. However, subtle concerns may be within the broad range of normal behavior or behaviors that will change in response to the natural contingencies of social exchanges once the client stops avoiding and starts entering more social situations. Finally, the therapist should consider whether safety behaviors may be masquerading as poor skills. For example, a client may make poor eye contact when he is anxious because it helps reduce anxiety but he knows he should make better eye contact and he does so when not anxious.

Development of the Treatment Contract

For clients with complex clinical presentations, the pretreatment assessment battery provides more data regarding whether the client's symptoms are best accounted for by the diagnosis of social anxiety disorder and whether social anxiety should be the initial focus of treatment. Our preference is for clients beginning this program to make it the primary focus for an agreed-upon period of time such as 12–16 weeks, even if significant co-primary or secondary diagnoses, such as depression, are present. Otherwise, at particularly challenging points during treatment, such as the initiation of exposure exercises, it is easy to fall into the trap of switching the focus of therapy to other issues. In such instances, avoidance behavior is reinforced. Furthermore, we believe, based on clinical experience and research, that clients who do not receive a sufficient dose of exposure are unlikely to improve. Importantly, we do not want clients who have read the client workbook but completed few or no in-session or *in vivo* exposures to incorrectly conclude that this program did not work for them.

Assessment During Treatment

Assessment plays an important role in all aspects of this program. Clients are asked to complete a number of exercises to identify physical, cognitive, and behavioral symptoms of anxiety, and to identify automatic thoughts and associated emotions and thinking errors, as described throughout the client workbook and this therapist guide. Beginning in the third session, we ask clients to complete the Social Anxiety Session Change Index (SASCI; Hayes, Miller, Hope, Heimberg, & Juster, 2008) each week, and the therapist and the client graph these weekly scores together to collaboratively monitor the client's progress. The SASCI (in chapter 3 of the client workbook) is a 4-item scale that asks clients to indicate how much they feel that they have changed from the beginning of therapy on four dimensions: anxiety, avoidance, concern about humiliation and embarrassment, and interference. A total score of 16 indicates no change since the beginning of treatment. Scores of 4–15 indicate improvement while scores of 17–28 indicate deterioration. The internal consistency of the SASCI across sessions is good, with alphas ranging from 0.84 to 0.94. In the study by Hayes et al. (2008), changes on the SASCI were related to changes in fear of negative evaluation and to clinician-rated improvement in social anxiety, but not to depression or anxiety sensitivity. Vignettes describing the use of the SASCI with clients demonstrating different patterns of change are provided by Hayes et al. (2008). There is substantial variability in the pattern and rate of change on the SASCI, even with successful outcomes. Therapists should be aware that many clients show little change on the SASCI in the first few administrations but that the overall pattern after that should reflect a reduction in scores. As *in vivo* exposures become more challenging, SASCI scores might temporarily worsen as anxiety increases in response to these challenges. Therapists should be particularly mindful of scores that reflect an overall worsening of symptoms, especially over more than a session or two, as such scores do not appear to be associated with successful outcomes. If the client also appears depressed or dysphoric at pretreatment assessment, it may also be wise to administer the BDI-II on a weekly basis.

Posttreatment Assessment

After the course of treatment initially contracted with the client, the assessment battery delivered at pretreatment should be repeated (i.e., self-report questionnaires, clinician-administered instruments, behavior test). The posttreatment assessment informs decisions regarding whether the client is ready to discontinue treatment, whether more sessions focusing on social anxiety are necessary, or whether supplemental or alternative treatments need to be considered.

At the end of 12–16 sessions, it is unlikely that all of a client's social fears will have been eliminated. In fact, elimination of social anxiety should not be the criterion for ending treatment. Instead, if a client stops avoiding key social situations, experiences a meaningful reduction of anxiety in a few areas, and believes that he can use the skills gained in therapy to continue to work independently, then the client is probably ready to stop treatment. Such a client is likely to continue to make progress in the coming months. Follow-up appointments are recommended to monitor the client's clinical status (e.g., 1 month and 6 months posttreatment).

In other cases, it may be apparent that treatment is working but the client's anxiety and avoidance are still too severe and pervasive for the client to be ready to continue on alone. This phenomenon is most typically observed among clients with generalized social anxiety and/or avoidant personality disorder (APD). It may also be observed among some clients who are depressed or have other significant comorbidities. In these cases, continued treatment is recommended. The data obtained from the most recent assessment should be used to guide decisions about the length of the new treatment contract and the domains that will be targeted during that time. The new treatment contract, as with the original one, should be for 16 sessions or less, at which point another posttreatment assessment should occur. For some clients, tapering of sessions over the course of the new treatment contract may be appropriate (e.g., meet weekly for 2 months, biweekly for 2 months, monthly for 2 months).

Lastly, in some cases, the assessment will reveal that treatment has resulted in little or no improvement. In some cases, the therapist may decide that the client's symptoms are better accounted for by another diagnosis, and the therapist should recommend appropriate alternative treatment. In other cases, social anxiety disorder may indeed be the primary problem but factors can be identified that have contributed to a poor outcome. Modifying these factors would become a priority. For example, environmental factors that promote continued avoidance behavior might be present for some clients (e.g., a husband who discourages his wife's increasing independence; an adult child whose social anxiety symptoms allow him to remain cared for financially by a parent). Therapy that addresses these environmental factors would be recommended before attempting additional treatment for social anxiety. In another example, overwhelming anxiety during exposures may be identified as resulting in poor homework compliance that has, in turn, contributed to a poor outcome. Supplemental treatments such as applied relaxation (Öst, 1987) or concomitant medication may make exposures more easily tolerated by these clients. Similarly, clients whose anxiety is partially maintained by the negative reactions that they elicit from others during exposures due to poor social skills may benefit from social skills training.

Culturally Sensitive Assessment

Multicultural competency is an essential feature of contemporary clinical assessment and practice. Although a full discussion of that competency is beyond the scope of this volume, there are a couple of issues that are especially important when working with individuals who present with social anxiety disorder. First, there are wide cultural variations in appropriate social interactions. The clinician must evaluate the social anxiety within the client's cultural context. For example, gaze aversion that might be seen as a symptom of social anxiety in European-American culture is culturally appropriate among certain Native American tribes (De Coteau, Anderson, & Hope, 2006). Care must be taken to not pathologize a culturally appropriate behavior or normalize a behavior that is unacceptable within the person's culture. Secondly, heterocentrism, the assumption that heterosexuality is normal or better (Herek, 2009), can impact assessment of social anxiety disorder. Therapists should be careful not to assume a client is heterosexual during the assessment process, especially when asking about dating anxiety. Until the client specifically indicates the gender of the person they would prefer to date, the therapist should keep their language neutral or ask specifically. A socially anxious individual who is also a sexual minority may be too unassertive to correct a therapist who assumes they are heterosexual, leading to potential withdrawal from treatment or an awkward secret that likely disrupts the therapeutic process. It should be noted that several of the standard self-report instruments for social anxiety also assume heterosexuality. We have ongoing research to develop better wording on some of these instruments, but for now, therapists can just discuss the specific items with the client and word them appropriately.

Session-by-Session Therapist Guide

Chapter 4 | *Overview of the Course of Treatment*

The remainder of this volume follows the client workbook chapter by chapter. In this chapter, we provide an overview about how to use this therapist guide and the client workbook most effectively. We also discuss a number of issues that are not particular to any chapter but arise throughout treatment including logistical details, encouraging compliance with homework assignments, development of the therapeutic alliance, time management in session, and pointers for the most effective therapist style.

Organization of the Therapist Guide

Each chapter in the client workbook has a corresponding chapter in the therapist guide, all following a similar format. Each chapter opens with a suggested time frame and logistical details about materials needed for the session(s). Thereafter, we provide background material that may elaborate on information in the client workbook or provide troubleshooting tips.

Detailed outlines for each chapter of the client workbook are available on the following Web site (www.oup.com/us/ttw). These outlines are designed to be easily used by novice therapists, who often bring these outlines into sessions with them. More experienced therapists may substitute their own vignettes for those in the client workbook and may rely only on the major headings of the outlines as cues.

For our research with the client workbook, we have established guidelines that our therapists must follow in order to be considered to be "following protocol." We hope that presenting our procedures in this therapist guide will facilitate the use of the client workbook in research and help others better understand the results of our studies. In clinical practice, these guidelines may be adopted more flexibly (Kendall, Chu, Gifford, Hayes, & Nauta, 1998; Kendall, Gosch, Furr, & Sood, 2008). Nevertheless, we recommend that these guidelines be seriously considered by all clinicians as a way of maintaining focus on the ultimate prize of therapy for social anxiety—termination of brief and efficient treatment by mutual consent with the accomplishment of mutually agreed-upon goals.

Our current research protocol states that a trial of therapy consists of 16 sessions of individual therapy conducted within a period of 20 weeks. All sessions are of 50–60 min, except the first in-session exposure session for which 90 min is recommended. The time frame of 20 weeks allows for missed sessions because of illness, vacations, and holidays without seriously compromising the momentum of therapy. Completing all 16 sessions within 16 weeks is preferred if possible. Prior to the 16 sessions with the workbook, clients have attended two to three clinic appointments during which an intake interview and additional assessments are conducted (see chapter 3 of this therapist guide). These pretreatment sessions, as well as the posttreatment assessment and feedback sessions, are not counted as part of the 16-session treatment phase.

Our protocol establishes guidelines regarding which chapters must be covered during the course of therapy. Therapists must cover chapters 1 to 8 of the client workbook, in order, without skipping any chapters. Based on our experience with the previous edition, we recommend that all clients cover chapters 9, 10, and 11 dealing with social interaction fears, observation fears, and public speaking fears, respectively. Although not all clients will have fears or need exposures in each of these domains, there are automatic thoughts, cognitive techniques, and rational responses contained in those chapters that are applicable to most individuals with social anxiety disorder.

The order of these three chapters may be varied so that the chapter most relevant to the client is covered first. Chapter 12, which covers advanced cognitive restructuring, should be assigned when the client is ready, often between sessions 10–13. When it appears that termination is near, chapter 13, which deals with finishing therapy, should be assigned.

To ensure that an adequate number of sessions are available to conduct a sufficient number of in-session exposures, therapists should spend no more than four sessions covering chapters 1 to 4 of the client workbook. Clients who are especially bright and motivated may have no trouble covering two chapters per session, so it is possible to cover this material in as little as 2 weeks. We do not recommend that therapists assign more than two chapters per week because, although they may read the material, clients will be unlikely to fully integrate it and make the most of the associated exercises. Therapists must strike a balance such that they are not moving so slowly that clients become bored but not moving so quickly that clients do not have sufficient time and repetition to fully absorb the concepts. If someone other than the treating therapist conducted the initial intake interview and pretreatment assessments, covering one chapter per session would give the therapist more time to work on developing a good therapeutic alliance, which is important for successful exposures.

Therapists should spend two to three sessions on chapters 5 and 6 of the client workbook. Because cognitive work is such an important element of this treatment, a third session may be needed for practice and repetition for clients who have difficulty grasping some of the concepts. The small minority of clients who, after three sessions, still have a poor grasp of the material are nevertheless advanced to the in-session exposure phase of therapy. We have found that a few clients are never able to grasp the cognitive portion of this therapy and that there is little to be gained from trying to force the issue. Heimberg and Becker (2002) make several recommendations for dealing with such clients. First, for the remainder of therapy, the cognitive portion of treatment can be de-emphasized in favor of relying more heavily on repeated exposure. Second, the complexity of cognitive restructuring tasks may be reduced for overly concrete clients such that they are given more realistic self-statements or a specific set of self-instructions by the therapist to apply in anxiety-provoking situations.

Table 4.1 General Outline of Individual Treatment in 16 Sessions

Week	Chapter in the Client Workbook Covered in This Session[1]	Activity
Pretreatment		Diagnostic interviewing and evaluation to determine appropriate treatment
1	1	Psychoeducational material, establishing rapport, and treatment rationale
2	2	Psychoeducational material, learning about own anxiety
3	3	Fear and Avoidance Hierarchy
4	4	Finish hierarchy, if needed. Psychoeducation about etiology of social anxiety
5 & 6	5 & 6	Learning cognitive restructuring skills
7	7	First in-session exposure
8	8	Second in-session exposure
9–11[2]	9–11 (as appropriate for the individual client)	Continued in-session exposures with one session devoted to cognitive restructuring and more elaborate planning of homework *in vivo* exposures without in-session exposure.
12	12	Advanced cognitive restructuring and core beliefs without an in-session exposure. May be expanded to second session if needed.
13–15[2]		Additional in-session exposures as needed with one session devoted to more in-depth cognitive work and planning of *in vivo* exposures without in-session exposure.
16	13	Evaluation of progress, relapse prevention and termination without an in-session exposure
Posttreatment		Posttreatment assessment and planning for treatment of other presenting problems that have not resolved, if needed.

[1]Reading of client workbook chapters is assigned as homework in the previous week.
[2]Expand to additional sessions as needed for more severely impaired clients.

Exposures should begin no later than session 8 and may begin as early as session 5, depending on the rate at which the material in chapters 1 to 6 has been discussed with the client. Chapter 7 should be an assigned reading prior to the first in-session exposure, the only 90-min session. However, a lengthy discussion of the content of chapter 7 is unnecessary, as many of these concepts have been discussed in the chapters prior to chapter 7. The new concepts introduced in chapter 7 are best demonstrated and discussed in the context of an actual in-session exposure.

Therapists may use their discretion in deciding when to assign the remaining chapters but one per week is common. When chapters 8 to 11 are assigned, therapists typically do not devote an entire session to discussing the contents of the chapter. Rather, they only address the content briefly during homework review and conduct an in-session exposure.

To be considered to be following protocol in our research studies, *a minimum of four in-session exposures must be completed. More commonly, the therapist and the client should expect to complete at least six in-session exposures and even more if possible.* Therefore, the protocol does allow the therapist the freedom to use a couple of sessions during the middle phase of treatment to do cognitive restructuring alone. Usually the first session without an in-session exposure happens after two to three sessions in which an exposure is conducted. These sessions provide an opportunity to summarize the work thus far and devote extra time to cognitive preparation and planning for increasingly challenging *in vivo* exposures. After more sessions with exposures, clients are typically ready for chapter 12 in the client workbook which focuses on the core beliefs, followed typically by one or two more exposure sessions. Our belief is that time is best devoted to repeated in-session exposures integrating cognitive restructuring. Table 4.1 provides a general outline of treatment, which is consistent with the approach currently used in our clinics.

Client Reading Assignments

The client should receive the workbook at the end of the assessment or during the first intervention session. We ask clients to read the chapter prior to the session in which it will be covered. The therapist is then free to hit the highlights of the psychoeducational material and work through clients' initial attempts on any worksheets in the chapter. Highly verbal clients may require little review of the chapter material and session time can be devoted to working through the material in a very interactive manner, emphasizing application to the client's own experience. Clients should refrain from doing the last assignment in the chapter that is labeled "Homework" until the material has been covered in session. This allows a final review of the material with the therapist before the client attempts to apply it. When the therapist reviews the homework in the subsequent week, he or she can determine if the client is ready to move on, based on performance on the homework. Homework assignments can be repeated as necessary for mastery.

Client Self-Assessment Questions

Self-assessment questions appear at the end of each chapter in the client workbook, with answers and page references in the appendix. We typically encourage clients to complete these questions after reading the chapter but do not discuss them in session unless the client has specific concerns.

Setting and Equipment

Most offices in which therapists customarily see clients are adequate for this treatment program. It is helpful if the room is of sufficient size to allow staging for the in-session role plays. It is extremely helpful to have at least one additional chair and some moveable furniture.

Having something to write on that both the therapist and the client can simultaneously look at is important. A blackboard, newsprint and easel, or white board may be ideal for this purpose. Alternatively, it may be possible to use a pad of paper on a clipboard as long as the therapist and the client can move their chairs so that they can look at and write on the paper together. Clients are often quite anxious in session and may have difficulty tracking information. Writing down key points facilitates accurate processing of the psychoeducational material.

Cognitive restructuring is greatly facilitated if the therapist can record automatic thoughts (ATs), various exercises for disputing ATs, and rational responses so they are visible to both the client and the therapist.

Agenda Setting and Ongoing Assessment

Therapists who are used to working with a less structured treatment are likely accustomed to a check-in at the beginning of session to see whether significant events have occurred since the previous session and to assess the current status. We accomplish this goal in three ways. First, starting in chapter 3 of the client workbook we ask clients to complete the Social Anxiety Session Change Index (SASCI) before each session. Therapists can quickly review the SASCI, plot the score on the graph provided in chapter 7, and discuss any notable changes, if needed. Second, cognitive-behavioral treatment typically starts with formal or informal agenda setting (e.g., Beck, 1995) for the session. For example, our therapists typically start a session with "I thought we would look over your homework and then discuss some of the material from the chapter you read. Is there anything you want to make sure we cover today?" By collaboratively setting an agenda, the client has an opportunity to voice anything she wishes to share with the therapist that might not come up otherwise. Third, the review of the homework itself provides another opportunity for clients to share relevant events from the week.

Therapeutic Alliance, Therapist Style, and Tone of Cognitive-Behavioral Therapy Sessions

A hallmark of cognitive-behavioral therapy (CBT) is "collaborative empiricism" (Beck, 1995). In this treatment, collaborative empiricism is operationalized as an active therapist and active client working together to overcome social anxiety. The therapist brings expertise about social anxiety and CBT. The client brings expertise about herself and the motivation to make changes in her life. At times, the therapist takes on the role of educator, especially when sharing the psychoeducational information in the early chapters and when teaching cognitive restructuring skills. At other times, the therapist is more of a coach or facilitator, helping clients further identify and understand the nature of their social anxiety, including cognitions and behavioral or affective reactions to anxiety-provoking situations. At all times, the therapist should model active involvement and encourage an interactive exchange with the client that is grounded in good supportive therapy skills. The therapist should listen attentively and always communicate empathy about the client's fears and concerns. However, such skills are often used to increase a client's experience of emotion and focus too much on the client's affective experience in the absence of active coping before an exposure may increase anxiety and make exposure more difficult. Ideally, the therapist will communicate that he or she understands that the client's fears are real and the anxiety may be intense. At the same time, the therapist should also communicate solution-focused coping that emphasizes using the material the client brings to session within the CBT model to help her make progress. By directly and indirectly communicating that clients are capable of facing their fears and that anxiety will be uncomfortable but not dangerous, the therapist helps build clients' confidence in their ability to stop avoiding. Later in treatment, greater exploration of affect may be useful to help elicit more central ATs and core beliefs, as described in chapter 12 of the client workbook.

Inexperienced therapists using this treatment tend to make two types of mistakes in terms of style and time management in the session: being too controlling or being too passive. One common mistake is to engage in extended lecturing about the psychoeducational material. Not surprisingly, many socially anxious clients are reluctant to talk early in treatment. An inexperienced therapist may simply take over the session and lecture, with little input from the client. This is a frustrating experience for both the client and the therapist and does little to build rapport. It also does little to facilitate the client's understanding of the material, as she does not have an opportunity to process it at a deep level. The alternative to lecturing when the client is quiet is to slow down and draw the client out. Specific questions that relate the client's experience to the material in the workbook are a good place to start. As the client begins to respond, good active listening skills, such as reflections and summarizations, can encourage her to talk further. It may take more time, but, especially during the first few treatment sessions, it is much better to move slowly and ensure that the client is applying the information to herself and the therapist is gaining an accurate understanding of the client's experience.

The second common mistake inexperienced therapists make with this intervention is to let the client dominate the session with long narratives about her experience of social anxiety. Traditionally trained therapists are often accustomed to letting the client take the lead and may encourage extended narratives by automatically using active listening skills such as nonverbal cues to continue (e.g., head nods) and clarifying questions and reflections. Any attempts to cover the psychoeducational material may be met by an extended recounting of how the material relates to the client's own experience. This style of session initially seems to build rapport as the client feels she has been heard and allowed to share her individual experience of social anxiety. However, it quickly becomes problematic as both the client and the therapist realize they are not progressing through the treatment as intended. Important concepts are missed so that later activities, especially cognitive restructuring and exposure, do not have sufficient background. Also, the client has been used to dominating the session and may try to do so to avoid anxiety-provoking activities such as in-session exposures. As the therapist becomes more heavy-handed to get back on track, the client, who is sensitive to negative evaluation, will likely conclude that she has done something wrong. This disrupts the trust between the client and the therapist and could result in withdrawal from treatment.

The Role of Affect in Cognitive-Behavioral Therapy for Social Anxiety Disorder

Cognitive and behavioral therapies have sometimes been criticized for ignoring the importance of affect in the therapy session. Although this view may have been justified in the past, it certainly does not represent contemporary CBT. In fact, CBT interventions for anxiety disorders, including this treatment program, depend upon the elicitation of anxiety through exposure to feared situations. The skilled therapist then guides the client in exploring the thoughts and images accompanying the anxiety, followed by reinterpretation of the meaning of the cues eliciting the anxiety and often of the meaning of the experienced affect itself.

For this treatment to be successful, the therapist must be comfortable with clients who may become extremely anxious. This may manifest itself as anger if the client feels "cornered" and unable to avoid highly feared situations (the "fight" portion of the fight-or-flight response). Clients often become tearful or experience shame as they confront their beliefs and share their fears about themselves. As gains are made and clients begin to see that their lives can be different, they may become very sad at the experiences lost to past avoidance. Less experienced or less confident therapists may feel uncomfortable with strong client affect and may try to help the client avoid or suppress the emotional experience. More experienced therapists assess whether the situation calls for them to help the client to experience, process, and accept uncomfortable feelings or use the uncomfortable feelings as a cue for additional cognitive coping.

Because clients can often have intense affective experiences, it is essential that the therapist create a trusting atmosphere and appropriate structure. Poor time management may result in insufficient processing after an in-session exposure or exploration of core beliefs. As session time winds down, the therapist must ensure that the client has sufficient time to discuss her reactions and then become psychologically ready to leave the session. Socially anxious clients are often not sufficiently assertive to request additional time to finish emotional processing and refocus their attention on the demands of their life outside of session.

Homework Compliance

This treatment program includes a homework component to facilitate transfer of gains from the therapy sessions to clients' daily lives. Homework varies from assignments to read a portion of the client workbook to *in vivo* exposure. Not all clients complete all assignments, but typically about 90% compliance should be expected. Although compliance with homework is associated with treatment gains (Edelman &

Chambless, 1995; Leung & Heimberg, 1996), these effects are not as large as one might expect. This may be because homework compliance is generally quite high in research studies in which several steps are usually taken to maximize compliance. In the sections that follow we describe strategies to encourage clients to complete assigned homework. We also discuss what to do if compliance is low. Therapists who do not typically use homework in their practice may find Michael Tompkins' 2004 book *Using Homework in Psychotherapy: Strategies, Guidelines and Forms* very helpful.

Establishing Compliance

Much of homework compliance relies on establishing its importance from the outset of therapy. The client workbook discusses the rationale for homework, and the therapist will want to be sure to discuss this as well. It is just as important, however, for the therapist to communicate the importance of homework with her behavior. This includes:

- Being sure that the client understands the rationale for an assignment and agrees to do it

- Carefully explaining the homework assignment and doing a couple of sample items in session, if appropriate (e.g., sample physical symptoms)

- Writing down the homework assignment, with a copy for both the client and the therapist

- Encouraging the client to contact the therapist if there is any difficulty understanding or completing the assignment

- Troubleshooting in advance likely obstacles (e.g., how to handle filling out forms at work or what to do if an intended conversation partner is unavailable)

- Making review of the assignment, based on the therapist's written copy, an important focus in the subsequent session

- Integrating information gained in the assignment into the session whenever possible

- Communicating pleasure with the client's efforts when assignments are completed, without communicating that this is surprising or out of the ordinary.

Although it may seem obvious that the client must agree to the assignment ahead of time, this does not always occur. The nature of social anxiety is such that communication about such matters can be difficult. The client may fear informing the therapist that she does not understand or does not intend to do an assignment. Socially anxious clients may be unwilling to say that the homework assignment is too difficult, or they may not report that they did not do it last week. The therapist must listen closely to what the client is and is not saying about homework with a supportive attitude that emphasizes the collaborative nature of decisions about homework assignments. At the same time, clients will quickly realize homework is unimportant if the therapist fails to remember the homework and/or fully incorporate it into the next session.

Troubleshooting Noncompliance

If a client fails to complete homework assignments after the therapist follows the guidelines to facilitate compliance just described, then it is time to move to problem-solving. Because socially anxious individuals fear negative evaluation from authority figures such as therapists, often briefly reiterating the importance of homework and addressing any obstacles will solve the problem. Early in treatment this should be done gently, especially for more severely impaired individuals who may become very anxious if they believe they have made a major mistake. If gentle reminders do not work, then the next step is for the therapist to express concern more directly and request the client's assistance in solving the problem. Again, this should include an exploration of any obstacles that are interfering with homework completion. It often also includes exploring the client's thoughts about homework and then addressing any automatic thoughts within the cognitive restructuring model. Noncompliance with *in vivo* exposure often results from avoidance behavior. The avoidance can be addressed with cognitive restructuring and/or breaking the assignment into smaller parts to make it more graduated.

Occasionally, clients, who are otherwise fully involved in treatment, do not follow through on homework assignments. If these assignments are not essential to outcome, such as completing certain paperwork, then they can be dropped. It is better to make more limited assignments that get done than repeatedly having a client fail to complete homework. The most essential assignments are the *in vivo* exposure exercises. Rarely is treatment going well if the client repeatedly fails to do *in vivo* exposures. Extensive and thoughtful cognitive restructuring records completed at home are no substitute for completion of exposures in the client's daily life. If this problem occurs repeatedly, progress through the client workbook should stop and all attention be given to helping the client face fears in her daily life. If this cannot be resolved, then it is time to reconsider the diagnosis and/or other intervention strategies as discussed in chapter 17 of this therapist guide.

Excessive Compliance

Clients who are doing very well in treatment should start to develop their own homework assignments and enter other feared situations during the week as opportunities occur. However, occasionally, a socially anxious client with core beliefs about the need to be perfect will perform excessively well on homework assignments. The therapist should be alert to this pattern if ATs about perfectionism arise in early in-session exposures. Reducing homework compliance to 90% may present an excellent exposure opportunity, following the discussion of core beliefs in chapter 12 of the client workbook.

Avoidance Within the Session

Individuals with social anxiety may have become extremely skilled at avoiding feared situations. This can manifest itself in therapy by creation of obstacles that interfere with in-session exposures. Some signs this may be occurring include difficulty with time management, repeated personal crises that must be discussed on the day an exposure is scheduled, arriving late for session, and repeatedly asking general questions about social anxiety or the treatment. If the therapist finds that there is not sufficient time to cover the intended material, particularly in-session exposures, then it is time to analyze how session time has been spent. Initially, it is usually best for the therapist to try and redirect the session around the client's avoidance. If this is unsuccessful, then the therapist should immediately but gently raise the possibility that the client is engaging in avoidance behavior that is interfering with her opportunity to make progress. It may be necessary to explore the client's ATs underlying the avoidance within the cognitive restructuring model before the client can identify and change the avoidance behavior.

Special Populations

A general discussion of multicultural competency is well beyond the scope of this volume. Hays and Iwamasa (2006) provide a good resource for cognitive-behavioral interventions in a multicultural context. Because of the wide cultural variations in social behavior, one general rule is that it is important for the therapist using this treatment to be familiar with cultural norms for social interactions if the therapist and the client come from different backgrounds. We have regularly encountered two particular situations that may be less familiar to therapists that we will discuss in the sections that follow: primary language differences and gay, lesbian, and bisexual clients.

The Client and the Therapist Do Not Share the Same First Language

All of the authors of this manual have English as their first language. However, we have often worked with clients for whom English is not their first language. Obviously, the client and the therapist must share sufficient common language fluency to be able to communicate about the important concepts in the treatment protocol. As cognitive restructuring proceeds, it may be important for the client to begin to do the cognitive work on the homework forms in their primary language. Even individuals with excellent language skills for daily life may not have as strong a proficiency in subtle meanings and the language of emotions that is key to the most advanced cognitive work. When covering chapters 5 and 6 in the client workbook, the therapist can indicate that it would be acceptable to do the homework in the client's primary language, if that is helpful. The client can then bring the homework sheets in and translate for the therapist in session. This discussion can be challenging because socially anxious non-native speakers may have fears of negative evaluation easily evoked by any suggestion their language skills are inadequate. Whatever language the client chooses to use in the early homework assignments, we have found that the later work on core beliefs is often best done in the primary language because it involves long-standing self-schema that were learned and stored in the primary language.

Gay, Lesbian, and Bisexual Clients

Several research studies have suggested that individuals who identify as gay or lesbian have increased risk for social anxiety disorder (e.g., Pachankis & Goldfried, 2006). Given that the lesbian, gay, and bisexual community (LGB—note some clients prefer the term *queer* to LGB) is more likely to seek psychotherapy than the general population (Liddle, 1996; Morgan, 1992), it is likely that therapists treating social anxiety disorder will see clients who identify as gay, lesbian, or bisexual. Although recommendations for general competencies in conducting cognitive-behavioral interventions with LGB clients can be found elsewhere (see Martell, Safren, & Prince, 2004; Pachankis & Goldfried, 2004; Walsh & Hope, 2010), there are issues specific to social anxiety that should be considered. First, it is important to determine the extent to which the fear is an irrational fear of negative evaluation versus a more rational concern about negative evaluation or significant negative consequences due to sexual prejudice. For example, a client who is afraid of speaking up at a meeting because others may detect her anxiety and perceive her as inadequate is very different from a client who is fearful of speaking up because of an expected hostile reaction due to others' assumptions about her sexual minority status. The latter fear may not be irrational and could have serious consequences for job security and promotion opportunities, given that in many places in the United States the lack of federal nondiscrimination in employment protection based on sexual orientation means there is no legal recourse (Human Rights Campaign, 2009). This suggests that cognitive restructuring that might focus on identifying the actual versus perceived likelihood of these consequences and examining the evidence to contradict negative automatic thoughts (e.g., Will absolutely no one like you if they find out you are gay?) needs to consider the local climate and realities for LGB clients. The therapist should recognize that there is the possibility that some fears, such as familial estrangement, loss of housing or employment, or hate-crime victimization, may be wholly justified and even adaptive in nature.

Other than considerations of sexual prejudice, as just described, much of the treatment can proceed as usual for LGB clients. If a client's goals include addressing dating anxiety, then the appropriate gender for the dating partner should be used. This requires the therapist and any role players to be comfortable role playing in this situation. Given the specific nature of fears, the therapist may need some familiarity with the local LGB community to assist the client in expanding her social network if social anxiety has resulted in extensive social isolation. This is similar to issues that arise when working with anyone from an ethnic, socioeconomic, religious, or cultural group that differs from that of the therapist. Although some LGB clients may prefer to work with a therapist who is also a sexual minority, we do not believe this is a requirement for this treatment to be successful. Regardless of their own identity, our therapists do not typically disclose their sexual orientation with sexual minority or heterosexual clients.

Chapter 5 Psychoeducation: Background on Social Anxiety

(Corresponds to chapter 1 of the workbook)

Timeline

Typically one session

Materials Needed

- Copy of client workbook

- Dry erase board

- Worksheet 1.1—Pros and Cons of Working on My Social Anxiety

- Worksheet 2.1—Physical Symptoms of Social Anxiety That I Experience

- Worksheet 2.2—Thoughts Related to an Anxiety-Provoking Situation

Session Outline

- Explain normal to excessive social anxiety

- Share the diagnosis of social anxiety disorder and the conceptualization of the problem

- Provide a treatment overview and give evidence for effectiveness of the treatment program

- Assess and enhance motivation to change

- Orient the client to an active role in therapy

- Assign homework

Homework

- Instruct the client to read chapters 1 and 2 of the workbook.

- Have the client complete Worksheet 1.1 (Pros and Cons of Working on My Social Anxiety), if not done in session.

- Have the client complete Worksheet 2.1 (Physical Symptoms of Social Anxiety That I Experience) and Worksheet 2.2 (Thoughts Related to an Anxiety-Provoking Situation) in chapter 2 of the workbook.

Therapist Note

■ *Clients should not complete Worksheet 2.3 (Monitoring the Three Components of Social Anxiety) and Worksheet 2.4 (Worksheet for Reactions to Starting This Treatment Program) in chapter 2 of the workbook and until after reviewing the material with the therapist in the next session.* ■

Overview and Appropriate Therapist Style

The purpose of chapter 1 of the client workbook is to help the client understand his diagnosis in the context of normal and excessive social anxiety. The therapist also helps the client gain an appreciation that cognitive-behavioral therapy (CBT) is effective and a basic understanding of the nature of CBT, including the investment of effort and energy required. Additionally, the therapist works to enhance motivation for change and build the therapeutic alliance. It is essential that the therapist work to build an interactive style in the first session to set the tone for the rest of treatment.

Therapists new to this treatment will find the session outlines at www.oup.com/us/ttw helpful. Novice therapists will likely want to take the outlines into sessions. More experienced therapists may need only the major headings and may substitute some of their own vignettes.

Socially anxious individuals commonly view anxiety as an all-or-nothing experience. Some people have excessive social anxiety and others—healthy people—do not experience social anxiety. It is helpful for clients to begin to think of social anxiety on a continuum. We often begin this discussion by asking clients about their thoughts about the various case examples provided at the beginning of the first chapter. At some point in this discussion, the therapist makes sure that the idea of social anxiety existing along a continuum is explicitly presented.

Normal social anxiety includes a degree of anticipatory anxiety before important events. The first example in the client workbook describes Nicole, who is nervous about making a presentation at a managers' meeting on her new job. Most people would be concerned about making a good impression, and because it is a new situation, would have some doubts about what will happen and how well it will go. We encourage the client to help generate other examples of social situations in which most people probably experience some social anxiety (e.g., first date, job interview). It is often fun to suggest recent events in the media such as a movie star who talked about her anxiety while accepting an academy award. Given the right circumstances, even someone who makes a living presenting themselves to other people can be socially anxious.

For obvious reasons, clients are usually more familiar with the experience of excessive social anxiety. Nevertheless, it is often helpful to walk through a case example to highlight the cognitive, behavioral, and physiological aspects of the anxiety. In the example in the workbook, Cory is going to meet his prospective in-laws, a situation that evokes social anxiety in most people. However, Cory's reaction is clearly excessive. It also serves to highlight how others might react to one's social anxiety by describing the reactions of Cory's girlfriend and her parents.

The client workbook also covers an example of extremely severe social anxiety. If the current client is on the severe end of the spectrum, it is useful to review this case as well so the client does not have the distorted belief that he is the "worst case" ever seen. It is worth noting that in our group treatment for social anxiety, several members of a given group often confess to fearing that they will be far more severe than anyone else is. It is reassuring to them when they discover that this is not true.

By comparing various presentations of the cognitive, behavioral, and physiological symptoms of social anxiety, the client begins to understand that anxiety has multiple facets, ranges in severity, and is a fundamental part of the human experience that will be modified but not eliminated by participation in treatment. Although not explicitly discussed as such, this is the first step in breaking down all-or-nothing thinking about social anxiety. The psychoeducational material has an underlying role in cognitive restructuring by encouraging the client to consider information that is discrepant with his schema about social anxiety.

Sharing the Diagnosis and Conceptualization of the Problem

Depending upon the therapist style, more or less time can be spent on discussing what the diagnosis of social anxiety disorder (social phobia) means. Some clients who will benefit from this intervention may not meet official *Diagnostic and Statistical Manual of Mental Health Disorders, fourth edition, text revision* (DSM-IV-TR; American Psychiatric Association, 2000) diagnostic criteria but will have significant social anxiety. The medical model is ubiquitous in Western culture, so many clients expect to have a diagnosis or label for their difficulties. Many clients find it reassuring that there is a name for what is happening to them. It suggests that they are not alone and that there might be an effective intervention for their problems. If the diagnosis will be shared with an insurance company or other third party, it is entirely appropriate for the client to understand what the diagnostic label does and does not mean. Additional diagnoses are also briefly discussed.

The discussion of DSM diagnoses helps ensure that the client agrees that his primary problem is best conceptualized as social anxiety. If the client fundamentally disagrees with this notion, there is little point in proceeding further. The highest priority becomes moving to a shared conceptualization of the problem.

Quite often, socially anxious individuals will have a strongly held causal belief about their difficulties. Examples of such beliefs include "low self-esteem," "lack of self-confidence," or "lack of social skills." If this occurs, the therapist should acknowledge the appearance of disagreement while sharing that this is commonly how people understand their social anxiety. The therapist can express belief that this is the correct treatment for "low-self-esteem" by focusing on how it results in physiological arousal and behavioral avoidance of social activities. In the spirit of collaborative empiricism, the therapist can also explicitly promise to continue to consider the possibility that the client's problem is not social anxiety by seeing how well the client's experience matches the material in the workbook. If the client can agree to continue this "data collection," then treatment can proceed.

Occasionally, someone has had a humiliating experience from which he feels he can never recover. Clients may have an actual physical disability that cannot be overcome. In that case, the therapist must acknowledge with great sensitivity that some things may not be changeable and the goal will be to learn to function more effectively in social situations despite the past experience or defect. If the client can agree to this goal, then treatment can proceed.

Sharing the Overview of Treatment and Its Empirical Support

Once the client agrees that social anxiety is a problem, the next step is to outline the plan for overcoming social anxiety. The therapist needs to be fully familiar with the treatment as outlined in the client workbook and this therapist guide to answer questions with confidence. The specific treatment procedures will be discussed in more detail after the client has a better understanding of the nature of social anxiety. At this point, it is best to just walk the client through the table of contents in the workbook. The therapist can point out that (a) early chapters (chapters 1–4) are intended to educate the client about social anxiety and analyze the client's experience, (b) the client will learn coping skills to manage the anxiety (chapters 5 and 6), (c) there will be an opportunity to practice coping skills in situations that are important to the client (chapters 7–11), and, (d) finally, the client will thoroughly explore closely held beliefs about the self, others, and the social world and prepare to bring treatment to a close (chapters 12 and 13).

We believe that best clinical practice relies on empirically supported interventions that are conducted in a manner fully sensitive to the needs of the individual client. As part of that philosophy, we believe it is important to inform clients about the scientific evidence regarding the effectiveness of the intervention they are about to receive. For most clients, this discussion typically takes no more than a few minutes but is an important opportunity to educate the client as well as enhance treatment expectancies, which have been shown to be related to positive outcomes (Safren, Heimberg, & Juster, 1997). We typically share with clients that the approach used in this manual has been shown to significantly decrease social anxiety symptoms in multiple studies. Specifically, of individuals who complete treatment, 75–80% are rated by independent clinical interviewers as having experienced meaningful reductions in their social anxiety. We discuss how we do not believe that it is random chance that 75–80% of people respond and 20–25% of people do not. We emphasize that attending sessions regularly, doing homework, being willing to gradually confront difficult situations, and being open to new ways of looking at the world, other people, and oneself are factors that substantially influence whether or not someone becomes a "treatment responder" and that these factors are largely under the client's control.

In the sections that follow, we review several studies that serve as the background for the discussion of the research on treatment outcome in the client workbook. This review is meant to provide an introduction to the literature supporting this treatment to therapists unfamiliar with it. In some cases, the therapist may also find it helpful to share this information with the client as part of a more detailed discussion of the efficacy of this treatment.

The first controlled study of the group version of this treatment (cognitive-behavioral group therapy [CBGT]) was conducted in the late 1980s. Heimberg et al. (1990) compared CBGT to an attention-control intervention consisting of education about social anxiety and supportive group therapy (educational-supportive group therapy [ES]). Forty-nine clients with social phobia (diagnosed by the criteria of DSM-III; American Psychiatric Association, 1980) were randomly assigned to 12 weeks of therapy in groups of about six clients. Clients receiving CBGT or ES improved both on self-report and clinician-rated measures and on most measures derived from an individualized behavioral test in which clients enacted an anxiety-provoking situation. However, individuals who received CBGT improved more at posttreatment and continued to be more improved at 6-month follow-up. A graph from the article showing a primary outcome measure, the 0–8 rating of clinical severity derived from the Anxiety Disorders Interview Schedule (DiNardo, O'Brien, Barlow, Waddell, & Blanchard, 1983), is reproduced here as Figure 5.1.

Approximately 5 years after the end of the treatment, we followed up with as many of the clients as we could find (Heimberg, Salzman, Holt, & Blendell, 1993). Ten individuals who had received CBGT and nine individuals who had originally received ES completed follow-up assessment. On several measures, including clinician ratings, self-report, and objective ratings of a behavioral test, the CBGT group continued to maintain gains and be better off than the ES group was.

The next study compared CBGT to phenelzine, a monoamine oxidase inhibitor (MAOI), at two sites in a randomized controlled trial

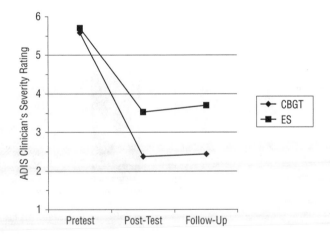

Figure 5.1

Clinician Severity Rating Scale Scores for Clients Receiving Cognitive-Behavioral Group Therapy (CBGT) or Educational Supportive Group Therapy (ES).

From Heimberg, R. G., Dodge, C. S., Hope, D. A., Kennedy, C. R., Zollo, L., Becker, R. E. (1990). Cognitive behavioral group treatment of social phobia: Comparison to a credible placebo control. *Cognitive Therapy and Research, 14*, 11. Copyright © 1990 by Kluwer Academic Publishers. Reprinted with kind permission of Springer Science+Business Media. All rights reserved.

(Heimberg et al., 1998). The design also included ES and pill placebo conditions. One hundred thirty-three persons who met DSM-III-R (American Psychiatric Association, 1987) criteria for social phobia entered the study. Both CBGT and phenelzine resulted in positive improvement across a range of measures that was generally greater than the improvement seen by individuals who had received ES or pill placebo. A key outcome measure was the percentage of participants classified as "responders," indicating substantial improvement or complete recovery. Although there was evidence that phenelzine worked more quickly, response rates were similar for CBGT and phenelzine at 12 weeks of treatment, as shown in Figure 5.2.

The design of this study included 6 additional months in which responders to either phenelzine or CBGT continued to meet with their clinicians once a month (maintenance phase; Liebowitz et al., 1999). The maintenance phase was followed by 6 months in which both CBGT and phenelzine were withdrawn. As shown in Figure 5.3, participants in the phenelzine group tended to be more likely to relapse after treatment

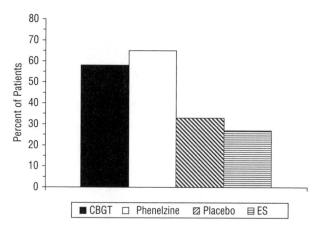

Figure 5.2

Percent of Responders at 12 Weeks for Clients Receiving Cognitive-Behavioral Group Therapy (CBGT), Phenelzine, Educational Supportive Group Therapy (ES) or Pill Placebo.

From Heimberg, R. G., Liebowitz, M. R., Hope, D. A., Schneier, F. R., Holt, C. S., Welkowitz, L. A., et al. (1998). Cognitive behavioral group therapy vs. phenelzine therapy for social phobia: 12 week outcome. *Archives of General Psychiatry, 55,* 1137. Copyright © 1998 by the American Medical Association. Reprinted by permission. All rights reserved.

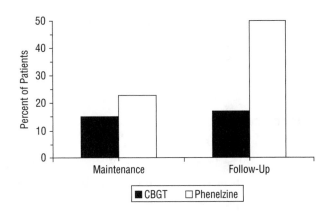

Figure 5.3

Cumulative Percentage of Clients Relapsed during Maintenance and
Follow-Up Phases. CBGT, Cognitive-Behavioral Group Therapy.

From Liebowitz, M. R., Heimberg, R. G., Schneier, F. R., Hope, D. A., Davies, S.,
Holt, C. S., et al. (1999). Cognitive-behavioral group therapy vs. phenelzine in social phobia:
Long-term outcome. *Depression and Anxiety, 10*, 92. Copyright © 1999 by Wiley-Liss, Inc.
Reprinted by permission. All rights reserved.

was withdrawn, suggesting the effects of CBGT are more durable. Other
recent studies have continued to support the efficacy of CBGT. In a
study by Koszycki, Benger, Shlik, and Bradwejn (2007), clients who
received CBGT were more likely to be classified as treatment responders
than clients who received meditation-based stress reduction training. In
a study by our group (Blanco et al., 2010), the combination of CBGT
and medication was superior to either of the therapies alone, although
this has not been the case in all studies (Davidson et al., 2004).

All of these studies investigated the group version of this treatment or
one very similar to it. Since the publication of the first edition of the
client workbook, we have completed a study that further supports the
efficacy of individual treatment (Ledley et al., 2009). We compared 16
sessions of individual treatment based on the workbook to a minimal
contact delayed treatment control condition. Individuals in immediate
treatment were substantially improved across a variety of self-report and
clinician-administered measures. As expected, those on the delayed condition neither improved nor deteriorated over the 16-week wait. The
treatment also appeared to be well tolerated as fewer withdrew from
treatment (less than 10%) than in most studies using the group format

(about 25%). At a 3-month follow-up assessment, gains made during treatment had been maintained.

Assess and Enhance Motivation for Change

The Pros and Cons of Working on My Social Anxiety worksheet in chapter 1 of the workbook (Worksheet 1.1) is intended to help the therapist assess and enhance the client motivation to change. Westra and Dozois (2006) recently demonstrated the benefits of addressing the motivation of individuals with anxiety disorders prior to treatment. A mixed group of clients with social anxiety disorder, panic disorder, and generalized anxiety disorder were randomized to receive either three sessions of motivational interviewing or no intervention prior to cognitive-behavioral treatment. Individuals who received motivational interviewing demonstrated significantly increased positive expectancies for change, had better homework compliance, and were more likely to be treatment responders. A trend toward better retention was also found for the motivational interviewing group.

Moreover, individuals beginning this treatment program will vary in terms of their readiness for change (Arkowitz & Westra, 2004), and it is helpful to address this issue directly. Some clients will start treatment in the action stage, ready and willing to do whatever is necessary to change their lives. Such clients should list any barriers to change that they can identify on the worksheet, but it is fine if the majority of the exercise involves having the client elaborate upon reasons for changing while the therapist makes statements supporting the client's self-efficacy for change and amplifying these reasons for change using reflective listening skills.

It is not at all unusual, however, for clients to start treatment in a stage of change characterized by some degree of ambivalence. Often, clients yearn for a different life but simultaneously have a variety of reasons that make them hesitant to take action to make changes. Using Worksheet 1.1, the therapist helps the client to articulate both reasons for changing and staying the same. Focusing exclusively on reasons for changing risks eliciting resistance, as the client may start to work harder to make the therapist understand arguments against change. To diffuse this potential problem, the therapist empathically acknowledges the difficulty of change and the client's perceptions of barriers to change. Additionally, it is important for the therapist to let the client develop the arguments for change. The most motivating and compelling reason to change for a particular client may not be the one that the therapist would have guessed. Moreover, the therapist does attempt to subtly sway the "decisional balance" in the direction of change by helping the client, through questions and reflective listening, more fully articulate the pain experienced from the problem and benefits of change, compared to the amount of time spent on arguments for staying the same. Said differently, the therapist helps clients become their own advocate for change (Westra & Dozois, 2006). For clients who have significant problems with motivation, a more intensive motivational intervention similar to that provided by Westra and Dozois (2006) may be in order. For a thorough discussion of principles and strategies of motivational interviewing, see Miller and Rollnick (2002).

Another goal of this segment of the chapter is to provide an opportunity for the client and the therapist to work together on a structured activity in an effort to enhance the collaborative, interactive nature of this early treatment session. In conducting supervision with new therapists, we have found that it is easy for them to fall into the trap of lecturing too much during this first session as they review issues such as diagnostics, treatment format, empirical support for the treatment, and so on. As stated previously, we emphasize using good basic therapy skills (e.g., reflecting feelings, summarizing, asking open-ended questions) throughout all parts of the first session and encourage therapists to make it as interactive as possible. However, we have also noted that a degree of structure, such as that provided by this activity, can go a long way toward enhancing the interactive nature of this session.

Orienting the Client to an Active Role in Therapy

Another goal of chapter 1 of the workbook is to socialize the client to the CBT model. An important aspect of this socialization is helping the client to understand the need for his active participation, including making an emotional investment in change and participating in the many activities of therapy. The goal is to help clients appreciate what lies ahead without discouraging them. Emphasizing therapy as a team effort helps prevent more depressed clients from becoming overwhelmed and discouraged by these demands. The primary message is empowerment. The client learns that there are things he can do to help overcome social anxiety. Empowerment helps overcome demoralization, the primary reason people seek psychotherapy (Frank & Frank, 1991), in the early sessions, until treatment has progressed sufficiently for the client to see changes in his symptoms.

Emphasizing the team aspects of collaborative empiricism offers another good opportunity for the therapist to build rapport. The therapist will be actively involved throughout treatment as he or she has been in the first session. By giving the client an active role in treatment, the therapist also communicates confidence in the client's ability to participate and make changes.

Chapter 6 — Psychoeducation: Understanding the Nature of Social Anxiety and How to Manage It

(Corresponds to chapter 2 of the workbook)

Timeline

Typically one session

Materials Needed

- Copy of client workbook

- Dry erase board

- Worksheet 2.3—Monitoring the Three Components of Social Anxiety

- Worksheet 2.4—Worksheet for Reactions to Starting This Treatment Program

- Worksheet 3.1—Brainstorming for Your Fear and Avoidance Hierarchy

Session Outline

- Review homework

- Explain the tripartite model of anxiety

- Explain the downward spiral of anxiety

- Provide treatment rationale

- Assign homework

Homework

- Have the client complete Worksheet 2.3 (Monitoring the Three Components of Social Anxiety).

- Have the client complete Worksheet 2.4 (Worksheet for Reactions to Starting This Treatment Program).

- Instruct the client to read chapter 3 of the workbook.

- Have the client complete Worksheet 3.1 (Brainstorming for Your Fear and Avoidance Hierarchy).

Overview and Appropriate Therapist Style

Chapter 2 in the client workbook helps clients understand more about their own anxiety in the context of the cognitive-behavioral model. The chapter closes with a detailed discussion of the three components of treatment that will directly address social anxiety. Homework involves monitoring the three components of anxiety and an assessment of the client's reactions to the treatment rationale and treatment components. As is true of all of the psychoeducational material, the session should be highly interactive, with both the client and the therapist playing active roles. When the therapist facilitates the client's sharing of her own experience in the context of the session structure, it further builds the therapeutic alliance.

Rationale

Much of the session is devoted to explaining the tripartite model of anxiety—physiological arousal, behavioral disruption and avoidance, and distorted cognition. The interaction of these three components underlies the cognitive-behavioral therapy (CBT) model for this treatment. Therefore, it is essential to spend some time developing the ideas with clients and applying them to their own experience. As clients become more sophisticated about the different aspects of their anxiety, the experience of anxiety becomes less mysterious and will be perceived as potentially more controllable. The material in this chapter begins laying the groundwork for cognition as the precipitating event in a downward spiral and for avoidance as key in maintaining the problem. These concepts are important for helping the client understand the rationale for the primary components of treatment (i.e., cognitive restructuring and exposure both in and out of session) presented later in the chapter.

The Tripartite Model of Anxiety

One goal of this chapter is to develop a common language to understand anxiety. We have found it helpful to spend some time on each of the three components of anxiety to ensure that the client understands each component before moving on to their interaction. Chapter 2 of the workbook includes several checklists and worksheets to aid clients in identifying experiences often reported by clients with social anxiety disorder. A recent anxiety-provoking situation can be elicited to help clients identify their physiological responses, cognitions, and overt and subtle avoidance behaviors. It is important to write down the examples generated for each of the components of social anxiety on an easel or white board so that the therapist and the client can view them together during the session.

The Cognitive-Behavioral Model—The Downward Spiral

Chapter 2 of the workbook presents the basic CBT model in the discussion of the downward spiral of anxiety. The chapter includes a vignette of Cathy, who fears asking for a promised raise. Using either this vignette or another one, it is very important to lead the client through the interaction of the three components, starting with an initial automatic thought (AT) that sets the tone. For example, Cathy starts with the following: "Something must be wrong with my work or they would have given me a raise." The working model assumes the primacy of cognition. Although there is evidence that affect can occur prior to or without apparent cognition under certain conditions (e.g., Izard, 1992), for the purposes of this treatment, all anxiety is considered to start with an AT.

In addition to the primacy of cognition, the second key concept to communicate is that avoidance has several negative consequences. Throughout the discussion, it is important to highlight the short- and long-term consequences of behavioral avoidance. Clients usually recognize that avoidance leads to an immediate decrement in anxiety, but initial relief is followed by negative affect including shame, frustration, and disappointment. For socially anxious individuals to stop avoiding feared situations, they must understand that the anxiety will eventually habituate and that they may learn that some of their worst fears do not come true. Therapists often find the graph in Figure 6.1 helpful in the discussion of the reinforcing nature of avoidance. We draw the graph on our white board, walking the client through step-by-step, typically using a recent experience that she has shared. We start by explaining how the graph works, drawing the X and Y axes and labeling them. Then we draw the line indicating what individuals with social anxiety expect their anxiety to do if they do not avoid—to continually increase as indicated by the line ending in the upward arrow. Then we draw the second example that depicts avoidance, with the vertical line to indicate when avoidance occurs. Clients easily identify with the idea that their anxiety would decrease rapidly at that point. Finally, we draw the third line on the graph, indicating that anxiety increases and then decreases in a habituation curve and present this as the normal course of anxiety as the body regulates itself to not experience excessive fear in the absence of actual physical threat. One of the biggest problems with avoidance is that clients never find out that their anxiety will eventually decrease. Many clients find this visual depiction compelling, and it

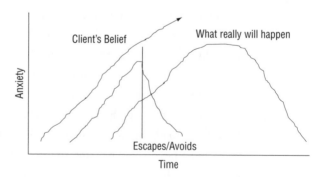

Figure 6.1

Rationale for Exposure: Patterns of Anxiety Response

can serve as a useful cue to avoid avoidance later in treatment. For many clients, it is a turning point in treatment once they have the personal experience that their anxiety increases then decreases in a predictable fashion.

Presenting the Components of Treatment

Once the client understands how the three components of anxiety interact to create a downward spiral of anxiety, it is important to carefully describe how the components of treatment (systematic graduated exposure, cognitive restructuring, and homework) interrupt this cycle. This discussion requires a careful balance of informing the client about the nature of exposures, yet not making her so anxious that avoidance of treatment becomes a problem. We usually share our slogan "Invest anxiety in a calmer future" to emphasize the fact that facing one's fears may create anxiety, but there is a positive long-term payoff. The notion that one must face her fears to overcome them is familiar to most people and part of our folk wisdom. The therapist can draw on the client's likely agreement with this principle while emphasizing that exposures are done very systematically. It is essential to make these three points:

1. Exposures will not start right away. There are at least three other sessions (and typically more) that must happen first.

2. Exposures are graduated, starting with easier ones and working up to the harder situations as the client builds her confidence with success.

3. Exposures occur only after the client develops some skills to cope with anxiety (e.g., cognitive restructuring).

The client workbook includes an analogy of learning to swim that we have often used for presenting the rationale for graduated exposure. A person can learn to swim by repeatedly jumping into the deep end of the pool and struggling to the side. After swallowing a lot of water and being repeatedly frightened, the person will likely learn to swim. On the other hand, one can learn to swim by starting gradually in the shallow end of the pool. First, the person gets used to being in the water and then may practice putting her face in the water. As the person gets more comfortable, she can begin to float and later paddle around. Although the person is likely to be somewhat anxious jumping into the deep end of the pool the first time, she will be able to depend upon the skills already learned and jump in with greater confidence. Both methods result in learning to swim. The graduated method may be a little slower, but it is definitely less painful.

The description of cognitive restructuring need not be very elaborate or cover all of Beckian theory. If the therapist has pointed out the thoughts the client has in anxiety-provoking situations and fully developed the model, then the client should readily accept that thoughts are an important part of her anxiety. Cognitive restructuring can then be described as learning a series of steps to look at those thoughts and see how helpful or realistic they truly are.

As with cognitive restructuring, the description of homework can be fairly succinct. Clients appreciate that they must learn to overcome their fears in their daily lives, not just within the therapy session. In fact, some are relieved that there is specific attention to transferring therapeutic gains to their lives outside of therapy. As with the discussion of exposure, it is important to emphasize that they will not be asked to face highly feared situations immediately.

Linking the three components—graduated exposure, cognitive restructuring, and homework—to the symptoms the client experiences via the CBT model is the final point in building the rationale for therapy. For example, the therapist makes sure that the client understands that cognitive restructuring targets anxiety-provoking thoughts directly, targets physiological arousal by decreasing perceptions of danger, and targets the behavioral component by freeing up more attention for the social task at hand and decreasing avoidance. It is also important that the client understands that exposures help her to practice the behaviors needed in feared social situations, help habituation to occur, and allow for a test of negative predictions about the feared social situation so that faulty beliefs may be corrected.

Frank and Frank (1991) list a shared rationale as one of the fundamental components of psychotherapy. The client and the therapist now have a common language to discuss social anxiety. As with all good rationales, this one points to a set of procedures or treatment techniques that are required to overcome the problem. These techniques, or the ritual in Frank's language, are another fundamental component of psychotherapy. Because of the importance of agreement on the rationale and ritual, chapter 2 in the workbook ends with an assessment of the client's agreement based on Borkovec and Nau's (1972) measure of treatment credibility. This is typically done at home and then reviewed in the subsequent session. Processing of the responses is described in chapter 7.

Worksheets and Homework

Throughout chapter 2 of the workbook there are worksheets that allow the client to record her symptoms. If the client is reading the chapter before the session, this recording can initially be done at home and then reviewed and expanded upon in the session. If the client is reading after the session, then the discussion can orient around filling in the worksheets after initial presentation of the concepts. In either event, the client should complete Worksheet 2.3 (Monitoring the Three Components of Social Anxiety) and Worksheet 2.4 (Worksheet for Reactions to Starting This Treatment Program) outside of session. This approach allows an extra opportunity for the client to think about and apply the concepts discussed in session without the therapist's guidance. This homework is then reviewed at the subsequent session as a check of the client's understanding of the material.

Common Issues That Arise

Physiological symptoms are the defining experience of anxiety for many socially anxious individuals. Symptoms often occur in anticipation of an anxiety-provoking event, during the event, or, less commonly, after the event is over. Many clients focus on only one or two symptoms. Occasionally, a client's entire presentation of social anxiety revolves around the belief that a specific symptom, such as blushing or sweating, is visible to others, with disastrous consequences.

In contrast to the physiological symptoms, some socially anxious individuals are often much less aware of their anxious cognitions. Often it seems that the thoughts are so ingrained that they are experienced as facts. For example, "I made a fool of myself" is not considered a thought by the client (e.g., "I was thinking that I had made a fool of myself"). Rather, it is reported as an aspect of the event (e.g., "That was the time I made a fool out of myself"). The best strategy is not to argue at this point whether a statement is accurate or not. Rather, the therapist can just identify potential thoughts in the client's narrative of a situation and record those on the board.

It is very helpful if the therapist begins to shape the client's reporting of ATs by recording the thoughts in a format that will be useful later for cognitive restructuring. In the preceding example, the therapist would write "I made a fool out of myself" on the board and verbally note that this is what the client was thinking about the situation. Similarly, questions should be rephrased in statement form. Statements better represent what it is that the client is afraid of and are easier to work with than questions in cognitive restructuring. For example, the client might report saying to herself, "What does she think of me?" The therapist should encourage the client to talk about the answers to that question that would be anxiety-provoking by asking "What are you afraid she might be thinking of you?" "For this situation to be anxiety-provoking, you probably aren't focusing on all of the good things she might be thinking of you. What are some negative things you are concerned that she might be thinking?"

Occasionally, socially anxious individuals will have very little awareness of their thoughts. Sometimes they can describe images of feared outcomes that can be translated into thoughts. Most of these individuals can become more aware of their thoughts through repeated self-monitoring in feared situations. At this point, just encourage continued effort. We will discuss later what to do if the cognitive aspects of the anxiety continue to be vague during cognitive restructuring.

Behavioral avoidance of feared situations is a hallmark of social anxiety disorder, but occasionally individuals will endure even the most anxiety-provoking situation without avoiding or escaping. Sometimes, these clients have little behavioral disruption as well. It can be acknowledged that the behavioral component does not play a major role in their presentation of social anxiety. If they are still anxious despite continually facing their feared situations, then it is likely that they are engaging in significant discounting of success. It is worth noting that clients who initially claim that they do not avoid anxiety-provoking situations do, in fact, avoid aspects of the situation. For example, if someone does not avoid parties, she may talk only with certain people, wear certain clothing that is unlikely to reveal anxiety symptoms (e.g., avoid sheer blouses that may reveal perspiration), or discuss only certain "safe" topics.

Such avoidance within social situations can also include "safety behaviors," which have been discussed at length by David M. Clark and his colleagues (e.g., Clark, 2001; Clark & Wells, 1995). When confronting feared social situations, clients may adopt certain strategies intended to decrease the likelihood of showing anxiety symptoms or behaving in an unappealing way. The client hopes that these strategies, the safety behaviors, will help her avoid disastrous social consequences. For example, the client who is afraid of her legs trembling during a speech may attempt to tense and lock her leg muscles to keep this feared event from happening. A client who is afraid of inadvertently asking a question that is too personal might never ask other people about themselves during conversations. Safety behaviors have a number of unfortunate consequences. Like any avoidance behaviors, they interfere with effective exposure in that what is feared is not fully confronted, interfering with habituation and new learning. Safety behaviors also tend to increase the likelihood that what is feared will, in fact, happen. Tensing and locking one's leg muscles may result in muscles straining and shaking. Never asking people about themselves during conversations may result in appearing socially unskilled. Therefore, especially for individuals who deny overt avoidance, careful questioning regarding safety behaviors is warranted.

During the explanation of the treatment rationale, sometimes clients will respond to the exposure aspect of treatment by protesting that they have tried to face their fears in the past and it has only made them more anxious. It is important to inquire about and listen carefully to what clients have tried before responding. Typically the therapist's response is that the exposures must be done in a certain way to be helpful. Usually the client's "exposures" were too infrequent or too difficult, or the person escaped when the anxiety became intolerable. In some cases, very reasonable self-paced exposures are undermined by cognitive distortions such as finding reasons to disqualify successful outcomes. Although clients may not fully appreciate how treatment exposures will be different from their own bad experiences, they only need to agree to withhold judgment until they have tried them. There are very strong data that exposure is effective for overcoming social anxiety (Feske & Chambless, 1995; Gould, Buckminster, Pollack, Otto, & Yap, 1997; Powers, Sigmarsson, & Emmelkamp, 2008). Regardless of what the person has tried before on her own, the therapist can state with confidence that these procedures are worth pursuing as they are very likely to be helpful.

When to Use Generic Examples versus the Client's Actual Experience

Over the years of group and individual CBT for social anxiety, we have developed a rule of thumb that it is usually best to first cover concepts with a generic example and then apply it to the client's own experience. This strategy has two advantages. First, anxiety interferes with processing information. Socially anxious individuals are more likely to understand concepts as applied to others, because discussing themselves evokes anxiety. Second, given socially anxious individuals' fear of negative evaluation, they may be quite ashamed when sharing their anxiety experiences or ATs. Starting with more impersonal examples facilitates learning and makes the process less threatening.

There are examples in the workbook to use for the generic cases in which to present the three-component model and the downward spiral. Therapists occasionally draw from their own experience as well. In the original group manual for cognitive-behavioral group therapy (CBGT), one therapist shared about anxiety in anticipation of a conference presentation that included physiological, behavioral, and cognitive symptoms. By having the therapist describe how her own anxiety began to spiral out of control, the client can see the therapist as a coping model. This can proceed without excessive self-disclosure and provides another example of how social anxiety is part of normal experience. Alternatively, a hypothetical example may be used. For example, in CBGT (Heimberg & Becker, 2002), patients work through an example in which they are asked to imagine a situation in which a person is in the lobby waiting to interview for a very desirable job. They are also asked to imagine that the person is feeling anxious and to consider what may be happening with that person in terms of physiological arousal (e.g., sweaty palms), thoughts (e.g., "She's going to know how anxious I am when she shakes my hand"), and behaviors (e.g., wiping one's palms on one's suit).

Chapter 7

Psychoeducation: Monitoring Progress and the Fear and Avoidance Hierarchy

(Corresponds to chapter 3 of the workbook)

Timeline

Typically one session

Materials Needed

- Copy of client workbook

- Dry erase board

- Thoughts About Starting Treatment for Social Anxiety form

- Social Anxiety Session Change Index

- Weekly Social Anxiety Session Change Graph

- SUDS anchor points

- Fear and Avoidance Hierarchy

- Worksheet 2.3 (Monitoring the Three Components of Social Anxiety)

- Worksheet 4.1 (Where Did My Social Anxiety Come From?)

Therapist Note

■ *You will need one copy of the Fear and Avoidance Hierarchy in session; two additional copies after situations are filled in but before SUDS and avoidance ratings are completed; and one additional copy after anxiety and avoidance ratings are completed.* ■

Session Outline

- Review homework

- Explain the importance of monitoring treatment progress and introduce and administer the Social Anxiety Session Change Index

- Develop an individualized Fear and Avoidance Hierarchy

- Assign homework

Homework

- Encourage the client to review first three chapters of the workbook, as needed.

- Have the client complete another copy of Worksheet 2.3 (Monitoring the Three Components of Social Anxiety).

- Instruct the client to read chapter 4 of the workbook.

- Have the client complete Worksheet 4.1 (Where Did My Social Anxiety Come From?)

Overview

Up to this point, the sessions have focused on psychoeducational material and building the rationale for treatment. It has also been a time to build the therapeutic alliance. By now, the client should agree that he has difficulty with social anxiety and have a basic understanding of the three components of anxiety: the physiological, cognitive, and behavioral. In this session, the therapist and the client review the client's ratings of treatment credibility (Worksheet 2.4—Worksheet for Reactions to Starting This Treatment Program), continue to refine their understanding of the client's three components of anxiety (Worksheet 2.3—Monitoring the Three Components of Anxiety), establish symptom-monitoring procedures that will continue throughout treatment, and develop a Fear and Avoidance Hierarchy.

Reactions to the Treatment Program Rationale

Frank has identified a shared rationale as one of the key components to successful psychotherapy (Frank & Frank, 1991). This may be particularly true of cognitive-behavioral interventions that require substantial time and emotional investment both within and outside of therapy sessions. If clients do not believe this program will be helpful in reducing their social anxiety, then it is time to address this problem before moving on. Our research with the group version of this program indicates that clients who are less enthusiastic tend not to improve as much (Safren, Heimberg, & Juster, 1997). We use Worksheet 2.4 (Worksheet for Reactions to Starting This Treatment Program) to initiate a discussion about the client reactions. Several types of client reactions will be discussed, with some suggestions for how to handle each reaction in the session.

Appropriately Enthusiastic

Over the years in our treatment outcome research, most clients have typically given ratings in the 7–9 range on the first three items of the worksheet. Scores are typically higher for the first item, because most individuals will agree that the rationale sounds logical. Expectations of improvement at posttreatment with continued improvement 1 year after treatment are also typical. These scores reflect overall investment in the program and some optimism that is tempered by an awareness that social anxiety causes major difficulties in clients' lives that will not be conquered in a day. In the session, these scores should be identified as "typical." It is also helpful to inform clients that their enthusiasm is a big step in the right direction to overcome their social anxiety.

Overly Enthusiastic

Occasionally individuals will circle all 10s on the first three items and give very positive ratings, approaching 1, on the scale for the expected severity of their fears after treatment. This extremely positive reaction should be explored with the client, without communicating that he has done something inappropriate by being enthusiastic. If the client is simply being effusive and is enthusiastic about starting treatment after an extended period of searching for help, then further discussion is not needed. As noted previously, inform the client that his enthusiasm will play an important role in the success of treatment. However, if the client sees the treatment as a quick and easy cure to long-standing social anxiety, then the therapist should explore these expectations further. Such clients may become easily discouraged if their unrealistic expectations are not met within a few sessions. Reminding clients that treatment is a process that requires acquiring some skills and gradually facing feared situations and that this process takes time and substantial practice may help inoculate them against early withdrawal from treatment.

Overly Pessimistic

Any ratings below 5 or 6 on the first three items or that show little hope for improvement on the last item of the worksheet should be explicitly addressed. These ratings suggest that the client may not be at all confident or invested in treatment. If a client is somewhat depressed, he may be willing to give treatment a try but may find it difficult to believe improvement in symptoms and changes in his life are possible. Other clients have tried many types of treatment without substantial success and thus may be skeptical that this approach will be any more successful. In either of these cases, the therapist should acknowledge the skepticism in a neutral, supportive fashion and ensure that the client is willing to give the program a try for some specified number of sessions (typically 6–10 weeks, with longer time frames for more severe presenting symptoms). Also, the therapist can remind the client that the research data suggest most people improve and there is no reason to believe he will not be one of them.

Occasionally the pattern of ratings suggests that the client believes this treatment program would work for someone else (e.g., it is logical and they would recommend it to a friend), but it will not be helpful for himself. This pattern should be thoroughly explored with the client as it indicates that the client believes that there is something about himself that is unique or impossible to change, representing a thinking error.

For clients with low treatment expectancies, it may be helpful to further assess the role of thinking errors by helping them to complete the following form titled "Thoughts About Starting Treatment for Social Anxiety." Some of the following questions may help clients having difficulty identifying thoughts and beliefs contributing to their low expectancies about treatment.

- What specific doubts do you have about this treatment program?

- What concerns do you have about whether this treatment can work for you?

- What are your worries about the exposures?

- What concerns do you have about your therapist being able to understand and help you?

The answers to some common concerns elicited by these questions appear at the end of chapter 2 in the workbook. The therapist should also provide educational information to correct any misconceptions that the client may have.

The therapist should use his or her judgment about clients' belief in the treatment rationale and proceed accordingly. Some skepticism is expected and probably appropriate. However, a general lack of confidence in the utility of the program for overcoming social anxiety suggests the program should be suspended until the client is more enthusiastic about proceeding on this particular course.

Tripartite Model of Anxiety

The therapist and the client briefly review the client's self-monitoring of thoughts, physiological reactions, and behaviors during an anxiety-provoking situation from the past week (Worksheet 2.3). Review of this homework assignment is an opportunity to reinforce the basics of the CBT model reviewed last session. For example, the therapist may point out how understandable the client's anxiety was, given all

Thoughts About Starting Treatment for Social Anxiety

As I think about starting this treatment program, I am thinking about . . .

1.

2.

3.

4.

5.

6.

7.

8.

Emotions you feel as you think these thoughts. (circle all that apply)
anxious/nervous, angry, frustrated, sad, irritated, embarrassed, shamed, hateful, other _____

Thoughts about starting this treatment program. Adapted from Hope, D. A., Heimberg, R. G., Juster, H. R., & Turk, C. L. (2000). *Managing Social Anxiety: A cognitive behavioral approach, client workbook.* p. 76. Copyright © 2000 by Oxford University Press. Reprinted by permission. All rights reserved.

of the thoughts that came up. If avoidance was one aspect of the client's response, the therapist may empathically help the client make sense of how avoidance was reinforced by short-term "benefits" but should also point out that there were negative consequences over the longer term. At this point, the therapist does not push the client to change his thoughts or behaviors. The therapist is simply helping the client see the role of thoughts and avoidance behaviors in his problematic anxiety. Encouraging the client to confront previously avoided situations or change his thinking during the homework review is likely to be counterproductive at this point in treatment, given that the client does not yet understand the principles of effective exposure and does not yet have cognitive restructuring skills.

Nevertheless, having heard the treatment rationale, some clients will arrive at this session with a description of their experience confronting a feared social situation that they had been avoiding for a long time. Therapists have the luxury of hearing how the client's attempt at exposure went before responding. For situations that went well, which is often the case, it is an opportunity to point out how the anxiety-provoking thoughts prior to the event did not accurately predict the outcome and point out other benefits of overcoming avoidance. For situations that did not go well, clients may not only be discouraged by the negative experience but may also use the experience as a basis for a belief that this treatment will not work for them. In this case, the therapist should emphasize that the client has not yet learned cognitive restructuring skills and the principles of effective exposures and that the client should withhold judgment on the efficacy of exposures until a couple have been conducted within session.

Lastly, it is not unusual for the client's written homework to have a number of problems with it. Although socially anxious clients are by definition sensitive to evaluation by others, it is important for the therapist to gently make a few suggestions for ways to make the homework more useful. If there are multiple problems with the homework, it is typically most beneficial to focus on the cognitive aspect and comment on the other problems at a later session. Sometimes the client will record questions (e.g., "what is he thinking?") that need to be reworded as statements (e.g., "he is thinking that I am boring"). Sometimes the client will have listed only one or two superficial thoughts (e.g., "I need to get out of here") and can benefit from assistance identifying other thoughts (e.g., "I don't have anything else to say"). Moreover, the therapist should actually write down the corrections for the client to see and have the client refer to the corrected sheet when completing the next homework assignment.

Monitoring Progress

From this point in therapy forward, clients complete the Social Anxiety Session Change Index (SASCI) provided in chapter 3 of the workbook at the beginning of each session. The therapist should make 14–20 copies of the form provided at the end of the chapter. The SASCI is a short, sensitive, easily scored, and easily interpreted measure with good psychometric properties (Hayes, Miller, Hope, Heimberg, & Juster, 2008). The SASCI is scored by summing the four items. A total score of 16 indicates no change since the beginning of treatment. Scores of 4–15 indicate improvement, whereas scores of 17–28 indicate deterioration.

It is recommended that the measure be scored immediately after administration, and the score entered on a copy of the Weekly Social Anxiety Session Change Graph, provided at the end of the chapter. The SASCI is intended to quickly alert the therapist to changes that have occurred over the week, and the therapist may choose to explore the reasons for such changes (or lack of change) with the client. This approach allows the therapist to deal with emerging problems, increase time spent on things that have proven helpful in earlier sessions, and otherwise adapt therapy in a clinically sensitive manner. By graphing weekly changes, the therapist and the client have an objective method of monitoring treatment progress.

Depression commonly occurs with social anxiety disorder (Magee, Eaton, Wittchen, McGonagle, & Kessler, 1996; Schneier, Johnson, Hornig, Liebowitz, & Weissman, 1992), and comorbid mood disorders are more strongly associated with impairment than comorbid anxiety disorders (Erwin, Heimberg, Juster, & Mindlin, 2002). Therefore, for our depressed clients, we routinely administer the Beck Depression Inventory—Second Edition (BDI-II; Beck, Steer, & Brown, 1996) on a weekly basis along with the SASCI. For many clients, improvements in depression will occur as progress is made on social anxiety symptoms. However, the BDI-II allows the therapist to monitor symptoms of depression so that a pattern of significantly worsening mood symptoms can be readily identified and addressed if needed.

All remaining sessions begin with administration of the SASCI (and BDI-II for depressed clients) prior to reviewing assigned homework.

Fear and Avoidance Hierarchy

Definition and Purpose

A Fear and Avoidance Hierarchy is a "top 10" list of situations in which the client experiences social anxiety. The greatest fear is in the No. 1 position. Items on the hierarchy may reflect variations on a general theme such as conversations with different types of people, or the items may consist of various situations such as public speaking, conversations, dating, and assertion. The hierarchy is an ideographic measure in that it is constructed on an individual basis with each client. Once the items are generated, each one is rated for the level of anxiety it evokes and the likelihood that the person would avoid the situation if it were to occur in his life.

In this program, the Fear and Avoidance Hierarchy serves three purposes. First, construction of the hierarchy assists the therapist in understanding what makes a situation more or less anxiety-provoking for the client. This is very helpful with later planning of exposures. Second, the hierarchy implicitly guides goal setting by identifying situations in which the client would like to be less anxious. Third, the hierarchy serves as an ideographic measure of treatment outcome when the fear and avoidance ratings are repeated later in treatment. These later ratings are helpful in making decisions such as when to end the program and provide strong evidence of the benefits of clients' hard work.

Instructions for Constructing a Fear and Avoidance Hierarchy

Clinicians unfamiliar with hierarchies will find most of the information about how to create a Fear and Avoidance Hierarchy in the step-by-step procedure outlined in the client workbook. The session outline (available on the Web site—www.oup.com/us/ttw) will also serve as a helpful in-session guide for novice cognitive-behavioral therapists. Here we provide some additional background information and troubleshooting.

Step 1: Brainstorming

The first step is to brainstorm a list of potential situations. The client began this effort with a homework assignment given in the previous session (Worksheet 3.1—Brainstorming for Your Fear and Avoidance Hierarchy). However, the therapist needs to be ready to supplement the client's work with situations discussed in previous sessions or identified as problematic during the intake assessment. Although the client will have generated some items on the worksheet provided for brainstorming, it is helpful to create a new list together on a white board or easel during session so both the therapist and the client can easily view it. As with all brainstorming, listing a range of situations even if they may not be on the final list helps ensure that all relevant situations are considered. The focus should be on situations in which the client experiences *social* anxiety. Clients with multiple anxiety disorders may tend to list situations that will not be appropriate to address in this treatment. For example, the individual with comorbid obsessive-compulsive disorder may fear contamination from eating in restaurants but have no social fears in this domain. These situations should not appear on the Fear and Avoidance Hierarchy for this treatment program. Additionally, clients will occasionally incorporate automatic thoughts into the situations that they suggest for the hierarchy. For example, a client may suggest an item such as "making a fool out of myself in front of my boss" as an anxiety-provoking situation. The therapist would help the client shape the item into one that lacks emotionally charged language (e.g., "fool") and is specific enough that it could be confronted in an exposure (e.g., "talking to my boss" and "making a mistake in work that I turn in to my boss" would be better hierarchy items). The situations listed during brainstorming can refer to a specific event (e.g., "attend high school reunion") or a general category (e.g., "conversations with strangers"). Often the more general categories are broken down in the next step. It is essential to include situations that evoke mild as well as more severe anxiety in order to identify easier situations with which to begin therapeutic exposures. A list of potential social situations, phrased appropriately for a Fear and Avoidance Hierarchy, appears in Figure 3.1 in the workbook.

Step 2: Discovering the Dimensions That Make a Situation Easier and Harder

Once an initial list of situations has been generated, the client and the therapist consider which dimensions or constructs make the more general situations on the list more or less anxiety-provoking. The primary purpose of this step is to allow the therapist to later predict how anxious the client will become during an exposure. By understanding the dimensions that affect a client's fear, the therapist can gauge exposures to make them more or less difficult as needed to achieve therapeutic success (Hope, 1993). Some of the common dimensions appear in Table 7.1. Not all of these will be relevant for a given client, and some clients have idiosyncratic dimensions such as the likelihood that a particular anxiety symptom will be visible.

Step 3: Fear and Avoidance Ratings

The next step in the hierarchy construction process is to make ratings of fear/anxiety and avoidance for each situation. This also serves as the opportunity to teach clients to use the 0–100 Subjective Units of Discomfort Scale (SUDS; Wolpe & Lazarus, 1967) that will be an essential aspect of communication during the in-session exposures. Education and practice with the SUDS ratings also provides another opportunity for clients to begin to think about their anxiety in a more complex, objective fashion rather than being overwhelmed by the experience of the symptoms and emotion.

Because of the importance of the SUDS ratings, the workbook includes an exercise to establish anchor points at the quartiles of the scale:

■ 0 = no anxiety; not necessarily happy but calm and relaxed

■ 25 = alert but able to cope; a little "hyped up" or "wired"

Table 7.1 Situational Dimensions Commonly Important in the Assessment of Social Anxiety

Characteristics of other person(s) present which may influence the level of anxiety experienced:

Familiarity

Marital status

Number of other people present

Socioeconomic status

Likelihood of future contact

Physical attractiveness

Gender

Age

Education

Power and/or authority possessed by the person(s)

Situational characteristics which may influence the level of anxiety experienced:

Structure (specific topics vs. "small talk")

Formality

Standing versus sitting

Anticipated versus spontaneous occurrence

Duration

Unique situational characteristics which may influence the level of anxiety experienced for public speaking phobias:

Question-and-answer session (including type of question)

Use of prepared notes

- 50 = anxiety definitely bothersome; some difficulty concentrating but still coping

- 75 = extreme discomfort and thoughts of avoiding or escaping

- 100 = worst anxiety the person has experienced or can imagine experiencing in a social situation

Although the scale is, by definition, subjective, these anchor points help ensure that clients use the full range of the scale and can be referred to later if a client's SUDS reports do not match the therapist's observation during exposure. Many clients essentially reduce the SUDS to a 10- or 20-point scale by using 10s or 5s only. This is acceptable as long as they are aware they can use the entire scale. Occasionally such clients will wish to communicate increasing high anxiety during an exposure by using the individual points between 90 and 100.

Avoidance ratings for the Fear and Avoidance Hierarchy use a similar 0–100 scale. Here the rating is of *behavioral* avoidance. Clients sometimes say that some situations are not avoidable, but this is rarely the case. Sometimes the cost of avoidance is extremely high (e.g., quitting one's job). However, if a client is entering a situation, then the avoidance rating should be less than 100. For situations that are not completely avoided, the avoidance rating will be more or less depending upon how often the situation is avoided and the degree of avoidance within the situation.

Avoidance within a social situation can range from obvious (e.g., the man who will only go to a party if there is alcohol so that he can quickly become intoxicated) to subtle (e.g., the individual who avoids ordering soup at a restaurant to avoid displaying a hand tremor). Avoidance within a social situation may include "safety behaviors" (Clark, 2001; Clark & Wells, 1995). Safety behaviors are behaviors that clients employ within feared social situations in an attempt to decrease the likelihood of negative evaluation from others because of some "catastrophe." For anxiety-provoking situations that are not completely avoided, therapists may inquire as to what catastrophe is feared in that situation (e.g., the person will blush, which will be noticed and then lead to negative evaluations by others) and whether the client engages in any behavior to ward off the catastrophic outcome (e.g., "I avoid talking about my education and career and steer the conversation to other topics; I try to get the other person to talk about him/herself to avoid being boring"). If so, safety behaviors are present and should result in a higher avoidance rating for that item. When exposures are developed, the therapist and the client would take care to not only confront the feared situation (e.g., conversations with strangers) but also include those aspects of the situation that are most feared (e.g., talking about one's educational background, revealing personal information). Ultimately, the client needs to confront the feared situation without avoiding any aspect of it. In some cases it may make sense to include hierarchy items in which the situation is confronted with and without the safety behavior.

As with the SUDS ratings, the workbook provides anchor points for avoidance at the quartiles of the 0–100 scale:

- **Avoidance = 0.** An avoidance rating of 0 means no avoidance at all. The client not only willingly approaches the situation but also fully confronts all aspects of it, even if doing so feels uncomfortable. The client does not engage in any avoidance or safety behaviors.

- **Avoidance = 25.** An avoidance rating of 25 indicates that the client almost always chooses to face the situation despite whatever anxiety he might feel. Even if the client puts off facing the social situation for a little while, he confronts it before any real problems arise. Within the situation, the client also might be engaging in some minor avoidance behaviors.

- **Avoidance = 50.** An avoidance rating of 50 indicates that sometimes the client chooses to avoid the situation because of anxiety. The client may also engage in avoidance behaviors while confronting the situation. Overall, a 50 describes a moderate level of avoidance that is probably noticeable to others.

- **Avoidance = 75.** An avoidance rating of 75 means that the client is usually avoiding the situation, leaving it early, or engaging in serious avoidance behaviors within the situation. Overall, a rating of 75 describes avoidance that is obvious.

- **Avoidance = 100.** An avoidance rating of 100 means that the client completely avoids the situation. Sometimes a person might completely avoid something that causes anxiety because it is easy to do. At other times, a person might completely avoid something, being unwilling to approach the feared situation even if it is very costly.

After all fear and avoidance ratings have been made, the therapist and the client should examine the range of scores. Clients with very severe social anxiety may initially produce a list of situations without items of moderate severity (e.g., all hierarchy items ranging from 85 to 100). Assuming that the client is using the SUDS correctly, the therapist needs to work with the client to generate items of lower severity before proceeding to the next step (i.e., one or two items should be as low as 50). It is OK if some of these new items are relatively artificial preliminary steps toward other feared situations. For example, a client with a severe fear of formal public speaking to a large audience could be asked what his SUDS rating would be if he reads something to the therapist while sitting down.

Step 4: Rank Ordering the Situations

Once the fear and avoidance ratings are completed, it will be time to rank order the situations, with 1 being the situation given the highest SUDS rating. For situations that receive the same SUDS rating, the situation with the higher avoidance ratings is ranked higher. When the anxiety and avoidance ratings are the same, it can be worthwhile to ask the client whether it makes sense to slightly adjust either of the ratings to break the tie.

The final version of the hierarchy should be recorded on the form in the client workbook. It is very helpful to record the situations first, make two photocopies for the therapist, and then fill in the ratings and make a photocopy of the completed form for the client. This provides clean copies without ratings to be used toward the end of treatment to monitor progress. Both the client and the therapist should retain a copy of the completed Fear and Avoidance Hierarchy with ratings.

Not all possible situations will be on the list. The Fear and Avoidance Hierarchy represents a *sample* of the universe of anxiety-provoking situations for a particular client. Like a good statistical sample, it should represent a range of topics and difficulty that is consistent with the client's goals for treatment. It should consist of situations that are presently relevant or could be relevant in the foreseeable future. Particular past anxiety-provoking experiences are not appropriate (e.g., a client dates the onset of his dating anxiety to a specific humiliating experience 5 years ago). Also, there may be current anxiety-provoking situations that are not relevant for a client. For example, many people fear public speaking but it does not interfere with their lives because they have little occasion to do so. In that case, public speaking need not appear on the Fear and Avoidance Hierarchy. Therapists should be cautious, however, that clients might consider some achievable situations as "irrelevant" because they seem unattainable. Clients may also be reluctant to include a situation because they believe it is committing them to an exposure later in treatment. In that case, the therapist can emphasize that the Fear and Avoidance Hierarchy should represent all situations they would like to address but that exposures are graduated so they will not be asked to enter a situation for which they are unprepared. Therapists should feel free to add or subtract situations from the list as seems warranted if a certain type of situation is over- or undersampled.

General Comments on the Fear and Avoidance Hierarchy

As can be seen, the act of constructing the Fear and Avoidance Hierarchy serves several purposes beyond simply yielding the hierarchy itself. The detailed discussion of various situations will be invaluable later as the therapist begins to design in-session and *in vivo* exposures. However, it should proceed efficiently. Clients or therapists may wish to engage in extended discussions about particular circumstances or the exact nature of a client's fear in a given situation. This type of analysis is inappropriate at this stage. When a particular situation is selected for exposure, the cognitive restructuring and exposure procedures provide ample opportunities for this exploration. Creating the hierarchy will typically take an experienced cognitive-behavioral therapist no more than a session. With less experienced therapists or very talkative clients, it should take no more than one and a half sessions.

Weekly Social Anxiety Session Change Index (SASCI) Graph

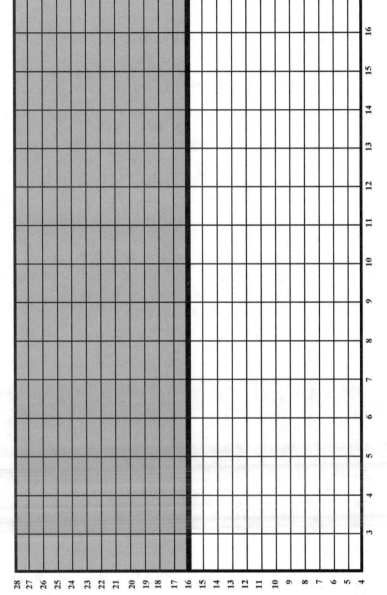

Session

* A score of 16 indicates no change since the beginning of treatment. Scores below 16 reflect improvement and scores above 16 represent a worsening of symptoms.

Chapter 8

Psychoeducation: Etiology and Development of Dysfunctional Beliefs and Information Processing Biases

(Corresponds to chapter 4 of the workbook)

Timeline

Typically one session

Materials Needed

- Copy of client workbook

- Dry erase board

- Social Anxiety Session Change Index

- Weekly Social Anxiety Session Change Graph (same copy as used last session)

- Worksheet 2.3 (Monitoring the Three Components of Social Anxiety)

- Worksheet 5.1 (Learning About Your Reactions)

Session Outline

- Administer, score, and graph the SASCI

- Review homework

- Discuss etiology and maintenance of social anxiety as applied to the client

- Discuss role of dysfunctional thinking and information processing biases in the maintenance of social anxiety

- Assign homework

Homework

- Encourage the client to review first four chapters of the workbook, as needed.

- Have the client complete another copy of Worksheet 2.3 (Monitoring the Three Components of Social Anxiety).

- Instruct the client to read chapter 5 of the workbook.

- Have the client complete Worksheet 5.1 (Learning About Your Reactions).

Therapist Note

- *Clients should not complete Worksheet 5.2 (Monitoring Your Automatic Thoughts) until after reviewing the material in chapter 5 with the therapist.* ■

Overview

The primary purpose of chapter 4 in the client workbook is to finish presentation of the cognitive-behavioral therapy (CBT) model with a discussion of the etiology and maintenance of social anxiety. Clients vary on how much they care about some of the details. However, nearly everyone asks about etiology at some point in treatment. The answers, as best we have them, are presented in chapter 4.

SASCI, Homework Review, and Agenda Setting

Begin the session by administering the SASCI and graphing the score on the client's Weekly Social Anxiety Session Change Graph provided in chapter 7. Given that exposures and cognitive restructuring training have not yet begun, little change is typical at this point in treatment. Importantly, therapists should not view administration of the SASCI as a replacement for checking in with clients about their week. Therapists need to remain aware of significant developments in clients' lives, remain attentive to the therapeutic relationship, and set an agenda for the session.

Next, as part of the homework review, the therapist and the client should briefly review the client's completed Worksheet 2.3 (Monitoring the Three Components of Social Anxiety). As in the previous session, the therapist highlights how the client's experience fits within the CBT model and notes any themes that are beginning to emerge in the client's thoughts (e.g., "I see that the thought 'I am blushing' came up for you again this week"). The therapist reinforces the client's attempt at homework and offers suggestions for improving it. If the client has done a good job reporting a few cognitions, the therapist might gently elicit a few more thoughts implied by the client's homework (e.g., "What are you afraid that other people might think about you if they saw you blush?") and write those thoughts down on the homework as well. Over the course of therapy, the therapist and the client will work together to develop a conceptualization of the client's beliefs about the self, others, and the world, and this process can begin by gradually helping the client to better articulate a variety of automatic thoughts during homework review and identifying themes in those thoughts across situations and time.

The primary agenda item for the week is discussing the research literature on the etiology of social anxiety and helping clients relate this information to their own personal experience. In the course of this discussion, the client's attempt at completing Worksheet 4.1 (Where Did My Social Anxiety Come From?) is reviewed. For some clients, this session involves disclosing emotionally laden experiences relating to the development of their social anxiety (e.g., bullying by peers, having an emotionally abusive parent, experiencing a panic attack during a speech, etc.). This type of self-disclosure is anxiety-provoking and emotionally evocative for many socially anxious clients, and therapists who use good listening skills to facilitate this disclosure can do a lot to solidify the therapeutic relationship in this session. This treatment does not propose that helping clients understand the causes of social anxiety will make the problem go away. However, helping clients make a connection between previous learning experiences and current expectations and beliefs about social situations can be useful in the cognitive restructuring process for some clients (e.g., "It is OK to be less than perfect despite what my father taught me"). Furthermore, the therapist has an opportunity to emphasize that the things that clients say to themselves and their behaviors are *learned*—and, therefore, they can learn to think and act differently through this treatment.

Etiology and Maintenance of Social Anxiety

The client workbook presents the biopsychosocial model of etiology. If the client has read the chapter, the research on each aspect of the model should not be reviewed in great detail. For example, it is sufficient for the therapist to note that research suggests that a tendency to be sensitive to new things or other people can be inherited. Conveying the notion of a "genetic predisposition" is important. That is, the therapist explains that, in the absence of certain life experiences, some individuals with a genetic predisposition to social anxiety never develop problematic social anxiety. However, this genetic predisposition, coupled with difficult experiences in the family environment or other important life experiences, can contribute to the development of problematic social anxiety. Moreover, because most socially anxious individuals can identify other people in their family who have similar concerns to a greater or lesser extent, some clients may believe that social anxiety is genetic and therefore cannot be modified. In such cases, a more extended discussion of a "genetic predisposition" may be very helpful. Although the absence of social anxiety may not be realistic (or desirable), more manageable anxiety with less disruption in functioning is a very realistic goal for all clients.

Therapists should use the questions from Worksheet 4.1 (Where Did My Social Anxiety Come From?) to help clients apply the material regarding genetics, family experiences, and other important experiences to their personal history. In this discussion, therapists should make sure to emphasize the ways that social anxiety appears to have been *learned*.

The discussion of etiology flows into how genetics, family environment, and important experiences can interact to result in deeply held beliefs about oneself, the world, and the future. Although not labeled as such in the client workbook, three dysfunctional thinking patterns are briefly described: external locus of control, perfectionist standards, and low self-efficacy. Each of these patterns is described in greater detail in the sections that follow.

There is a great deal of research showing that people who are anxious or depressed have an "external locus of control." That is, the person believes that something outside of herself determines what will happen. Persons with social anxiety disorder believe that other more capable and competent people control what will happen. In most instances, people with social anxiety disorder underestimate the control or influence they may have on other people's positive reactions to them.

Some socially anxious people set perfectionistic standards for their behavior in social situations. They also believe that other people's standards for them are unrealistically high. Along with these expectations is the belief that it is not acceptable for them to ever look or feel nervous in social situations. Other standards may emphasize never offending another person, always observing perfect manners, always being dressed just right for every occasion, or always being witty and charming. All of these expectations are perfectly admirable goals but unrealistic to expect of oneself on a regular basis. If achievement of perfection is the goal, one will frequently experience failure and feel bad.

Self-efficacy is the term psychologists use for self-confidence in how effective one expects to be. One type of self-efficacy refers to the belief that one can do something successfully. Socially anxious people often have low self-efficacy, meaning that they doubt their ability to do the right thing (or to do it well) in a social interaction. They may doubt that they have adequate social skills or the ability to make small talk. Sometimes individuals with social anxiety disorder also experience a second kind of low self-efficacy known as "low outcome expectancies." This refers to the belief that even if one can perform adequately (such as being assertive and asking someone to change her behavior), the person will still not get the desired outcome (i.e., the other person will not comply). Socially anxious individuals often expect that a situation will go poorly or that they will be rejected by the other person.

The final step in linking etiology to the experience of social anxiety in a given situation relies on the metaphor of the *amber-colored glasses*. It is important to devote sufficient time to establish and apply the metaphor. Although information processing biases are well established in the research literature, this is a very difficult concept to communicate to socially anxious individuals, especially without communicating that they are to blame for being inaccurate in their understanding of what is occurring in social interactions. The very amber-colored glasses we are seeking to explain will lead the socially anxious individual to feel easily demeaned for being "wrong" or react with a defensive posture. By describing the amber-colored glasses as a natural outcome of a particular combination of genetics, family environment, and important experiences, the therapist can indicate that the way in which the client processes information makes sense; it just may not be functional. In some cases, it was clearly functional in the past (e.g., chaotic alcoholic household in which survival depended upon being alert to threatening cues), but it is less so now.

As the client comes to understand that the amber-colored glasses lead to a perception of threat in a variety of situations, then she will see that physiological arousal and behavioral avoidance are the natural consequences. Clients typically identify with the fight-or-flight response. Even if they are unwilling to consider that the social situations they face are not as dangerous as they think, they can acknowledge that believing they are less dangerous will lead to less physiological arousal and less behavioral disruption and avoidance. This level of understanding is the goal at this point. It will take substantially more work to address this cognitive bias. In fact, this is the goal of the rest of treatment!

Chapter 4 in the client workbook concludes with a few commonly asked questions with answers regarding the etiology and treatment of social anxiety. Clients will vary regarding their desire to discuss any of these issues in more depth.

Chapter 9 Cognitive Restructuring: Identifying Automatic Thoughts

(Corresponds to chapter 5 of the workbook)

Timeline

Typically one session

Materials Needed

- Copy of client workbook
- Dry erase board
- Social Anxiety Session Change Index (SASCI)
- Weekly Social Anxiety Session Change Graph (same copy as used last session)
- Table 5.1 (List of Thinking Errors)
- Worksheet 5.2 (Monitoring Your Automatic Thoughts)

Session Outline

- Review, score, and graph SASCI
- Review homework
- Identify automatic thoughts and the emotions they cause
- Identify thinking errors in automatic thoughts
- Preview upcoming cognitive restructuring skills
- Assign homework

Homework

- Have the client complete Worksheet 5.2 (Monitoring Your Automatic Thoughts).

- Instruct the client to read chapter 6 of the workbook.

Overview

Chapter 5 of the client workbook starts with a review of the SASCI and the most recent self-monitoring of the three components of anxiety and then covers identification of automatic thoughts (ATs) and finding logical errors in ATs. The overall structure of the session, after the homework review, is to first introduce a concept with a neutral vignette, followed by an opportunity to apply the concept to the client's own experience. There are vignettes in the workbook, but therapists should feel free to substitute their own, as long as the vignette makes a similar point. As noted earlier, starting with neutral vignettes is helpful, because it allows the client to consider the concept initially independent of his own emotional reactions.

To assist therapists with little experience working with individuals with social anxiety, we share some data about the types of thoughts reported by socially anxious individuals in the context of in-session exposures (Hope, Burns, Hayes, Herbert, & Warner, 2010). We coded 1046 thoughts from 55 women and men into the 11 semantic categories shown in Table 9.1. Three categories, Performance (e.g., "I won't know what to say"), Negative Outcome ("He won't want to talk to me"), and Other-Labeling (e.g., "He'll think I'm strange"), accounted for over half of the thoughts. To our surprise, thoughts about the physiological symptoms of anxiety, visible or not, occurred infrequently. In chapter 12, we share some additional data from this study about which categories of ATs are best addressed earlier and later in treatment.

SASCI and Homework Review

Begin the session by administering the SASCI and graphing the score on the client's Weekly Social Anxiety Session Change Graph.

Table 9.1 Category Descriptions, Examples, and Distribution of Automatic Thoughts Across Categories

Category	Frequency (%)
Self-Labeling: Negative self-evaluation or label without reference to others ("I'm boring," "I'll be incompetent")	105 (8.86)
Other-Labeling: Concerns that others will attach a negative label ("He'll think I'm strange," "She will think I'm an idiot")	174 (14.69)
Visible Signs: Concern that the participant may experience visible signs of anxiety without mention of others seeing it ("I will blush," "I will stutter")	61 (5.15)
Other-Visible Signs: Concern that others may detect signs of anxiety that would possibly be visible ("She will see me blush," "They will see me shaking")	5 (0.42)
Self-Social Norms: Concern about violating social norms ("I'll say/do something inappropriate," "It would be rude if I interrupted")	53 (4.47)
Other-Social Norms: Explicit concern that others may see violations of social norms ("She will think I'm too aggressive if I ask that," "He will be offended")	15 (1.27)
Symptoms: Concern about experiencing anxiety symptoms that would not be visible to others or negative emotions ("I'll be embarrassed," "My heart is racing")	127 (10.73)
Past Memories: Negative thoughts about past anxiety-provoking experiences ("I always fall apart in that situation," "I have never been able to do that")	7 (0.59)
Performance: Concerns about failure to perform adequately ("I won't know what to say," "I won't make a good impression")	286 (24.15)
Negative Outcome: Concern that something negative will happen without an attribution that the participant caused it to happen ("He won't want to talk to me," "Not enough people will come to hear me speak")	181 (15.28)
Avoidance: Any thoughts related to avoidance, escape, or safety behaviors ("I will want to get out of here," "It will be easier if I don't make eye contact")	32 (2.70)
TOTAL NUMBER OF THOUGHTS CODED	1046

From Hope, D. A., Burns, J. A., Hayes, S. A., Herbert, J. A., & Warner, M. D. (2010). Automatic thoughts and cognitive restructuring in cognitive-behavioral group therapy for social anxiety disorder. *Cognitive Therapy and Research*, 34, 1–12. Copyright © 2006 by Springer Science+Business Media. Reprinted by permission. All rights reserved.

Clients will have completed another copy of Worksheet 2.3 (Monitoring the Three Components of Anxiety). This should be reviewed briefly at the beginning of the session. The cognitive portion of this form will be incorporated into the exercises later in the session. Therefore, if the form was not completed as homework, the first few minutes of session should be spent completing it. If it is necessary to help the client complete the homework in session, greater emphasis can be placed on the cognitions elicited by the recent anxiety-provoking experience than the other components of anxiety. This approach is recommended, given that the client will be asked to work with these cognitions later in session.

If the client has not done the self-monitoring of the three components or has done it poorly, then it is important to troubleshoot what went wrong. This needs to be done with a very nonjudgmental tone because socially anxious clients often react negatively to even minimal criticism. If the therapist works from the assumption that the client has done his best given the level of understanding of the assignment, then the troubleshooting typically goes well. See chapter 4 in this therapist guide for a more detailed discussion of handling homework noncompliance.

Step 1 in Cognitive Restructuring: Identifying Automatic Thoughts and the Emotions They Cause

Chapter 5 of the workbook opens with a vignette (two single men who greet a woman getting her mail) that introduces the notion that the exact same social event can be interpreted differently, resulting in very different outcomes. Neither interpretation is "correct" based on the available data. The contrasting interpretations do differ in their functionality. Only one interpretation results in approach behavior and possible further social contact. *The major point to make is that it is not events themselves that make a person anxious, but how one interprets events.* Clients are unlikely to be able to consider how their own thinking may be biased at this point. Therefore, it is better to stick with the neutral vignettes and work toward application to their own situation.

The second vignette in chapter 5 of the workbook (José and his thoughts about approaching a new manager at a party) is used to introduce:

1. Identification of ATs

2. A review of the downward spiral of the interaction of cognitive, physiological, and behavioral components of social anxiety

3. The consideration that the ATs may not be established facts, including how others might react if they knew what the anxious person were thinking

The therapist can present the initial vignette and then elicit possible cognitions and physiological and behavioral responses from the client. It is not essential that the client's suggestions match the workbook example. The therapist can suggest additional points as needed to fill out the vignette. If the client appears to need additional practice, there is a second vignette about Susan and her fears of public speaking in the workbook that can be reviewed before proceeding to the client's own ATs.

The notion of ATs will be used extensively throughout treatment. Therefore, it is useful to spend a few minutes carefully defining the concept. Based on the two (or three) previous vignettes, the therapist can point out how changing the ATs would have changed the person's anxiety level and possibly the outcome. Clients will typically be quite resistant to any discussion at this point of changing their own thoughts, so it is usually best to stick with the vignettes and talk about the client's thoughts in general terms (e.g., "One of your ATs is 'I don't know what to say.' If you were able to be less worried about what to say in conversations, you might be less anxious").

Two misconceptions commonly arise about ATs. The first is that the solution is to replace bad thoughts with good ones. Clients have often been exposed to affirmations and believe cognitive restructuring will involve repeatedly making positive self-statements. Affirmations are not cognitive restructuring. In the spirit of collaborative empiricism, the therapist should not suggest that the client's thoughts are wrong. Rather, the process of cognitive restructuring is one of mutual discovery of how helpful and logical the ATs are (or are not). The client should move from accepting the ATs as established facts to questioning them. The next step is NOT blindly accepting the opposite of the AT as a blanket positive affirmation.

The second misconception about ATs is that the client should learn to suppress the "bad thoughts." Wegner's (1994) work on ironic suppression shows that trying not to think of a certain idea (the white bear in Wegner's study) increases the intensity and frequency of its occurrence.

In other words, trying to suppress ATs will have the undesired effect of increasing their frequency.

Once the client has a basic understanding of ATs, even if he is unconvinced of the irrationality of his own thoughts, then the focus turns to identifying the client's own ATs. We have typically used the example of ATs about starting treatment, but another situation could be selected as well. The topic is less important than is encouraging clients to share their thoughts. It is helpful to write the ATs on the board with the therapist gently shaping the format of the ATs. Later cognitive restructuring works best with simple declarative statements. Sentences with multiple clauses should be broken up, and questions should be reformatted. It is always essential to check with the client to ensure that the meaning is retained after any gentle therapist editing. Here are some examples of appropriate therapist editing for ATs related to an upcoming meeting with a new boyfriend's family:

Before: *What if they don't like me?*

After: *They won't like me.*

Before: *If I don't meet their approval, Joe won't want to be with me.*

After: *I won't meet their approval. Joe won't want to be with me.*

In our experience, ATs in the form of questions often hide absolute statements that the person is not yet willing to own. In the preceding example, "What if they don't like me?" may be related to the client's deep-seated fears about being liked and accepted by others, as indicated by the revised AT. Sometimes the client prefers a less absolute phrasing such as "They might not like me." At this point, it is best to simply go with the client's preferred interpretation. Later, it might be appropriate to challenge the client and ask whether the more absolute phrasing of an AT is the most accurate.

Treatment is most successful when all aspects of the schema related to social anxiety are engaged and thus most open for the input of disconfirming information. Connecting the ATs to affect is essential for emotional processing and full elicitation of the schema. Any discussion of ATs should routinely include a query regarding how the client felt when he had the thought. Any affective material should routinely include a query about what the client was thinking when he had that feeling.

Step 2 of Cognitive Restructuring: Thinking Errors

The second step of cognitive restructuring, identification of thinking errors, is designed to label the logical errors in the ATs. As will be seen in the sections that follow, a few ATs lack logical errors but are maladaptive in other ways. One of the primary functions of identifying thinking errors is that it forces the client to step back from his ATs and consider them in an objective fashion. Although some effort is made to ensure that clients accurately identify the thinking error(s) in a given AT, if they can make a reasonable argument supporting a particular classification, that is probably sufficient. Most ATs contain more than one thinking error and clients' application of the thinking errors often reveals useful information about the personal meaning of a common AT.

In group therapy, we typically present each thinking error with a brief description and an example. This can be quite tedious in individual therapy. Therefore, it is best to explain the general concept and then highlight a couple of the most common thinking errors (e.g., all-or-nothing thinking and fortune telling) with examples. For clients who have read chapter 5 of the workbook in advance of the session, an alternative approach is to explain the general concept and then have clients explain which thinking errors seemed to fit with their experiences the most and why. The last category in Table 5.1 in the workbook, Unproductive and Unhelpful Thoughts, should be specifically highlighted as well. In particular, we typically emphasize that if other thinking errors can be applied to an AT, then that AT may not best be labeled as an example of unproductive and unhelpful thinking. Clients with a great deal of belief in their ATs may attempt to use this category to the exclusion of others that do more to advance the notion that a logical error or interpretation bias is present in the thought (e.g., insisting that a thought such as "Everyone thought that I looked foolish" is true but anxiety-provoking rather than an example of labeling, mind reading, etc.). Further, true examples of unproductive and unhelpful thinking (e.g., "I have never asked someone on a date before" [if that is truly the case for the client]) may be superficial thoughts that can be followed up with questions to get at what the client really fears (e.g., "What is anxiety-provoking about that?"). The answers to such questions often reveal new ATs with obvious thinking errors (e.g., "I don't know the right way to ask her" or "She will be able to tell that I'm new at this and judge me negatively for being so inexperienced").

As the client and the therapist practice categorizing ATs from a vignette (Beth and her job interview or a vignette of the therapist's choosing), the therapist can give the client time to read through the descriptions to find the right one. Although clients who fear making mistakes or are very anxious in the session may be hesitant at first, most clients grasp the general concept fairly quickly. If the client is having difficulty, try encouragement and gentle guidance (e.g., "I was thinking catastro-phizing might fit this thought. Can you see how that might work?"). If the client seems to be exclusively relying on one or two thinking errors to describe a variety of thoughts, it may be helpful to suggest others that may apply as well to encourage the client to think flexibly about ATs.

The next step is to work with clients to identify the thinking errors that characterize the ATs they recorded as part of their homework assign-ment from the previous session (Worksheet 2.3—Monitoring the Three Components of Anxiety). Most clients take readily to this, but in gen-eral clients are more hesitant to apply thinking errors to their own ATs than to the ATs in the vignette. Sometimes it is helpful to use the "as if" approach: "If there were a thinking error in this thought, what might it be?" This diffuses clients' concerns that their thinking is some-how "wrong." Again, the therapist can provide gentle suggestions for struggling clients.

Teaching thinking errors is greatly facilitated by therapist expertise in using the categories. Therapists new to this approach will want to study pages 86–95 in the workbook carefully to fully understand the categories of thinking errors. It is also helpful to consider the ATs commonly reported by a client in previous sessions and how these ATs might be categorized. Throughout the workbook are various lists of com-mon ATs and that discussion typically includes examples of thinking errors.

Previewing Coming Cognitive Restructuring Skills

This session highlights the first two of the four steps of cognitive restructuring: (1) identification of ATs and the emotions they cause and (2) examination of thinking errors in ATs. Next, the therapist, and the client if possible, previews the next steps by "talking back" to the ATs. Inexperienced therapists can rely on the disputing questions (Worksheet 6.1 in the workbook) to demonstrate how to challenge ATs. There is also rational rebuttal on page 116 of the workbook for the vignette of Susan, the anxious public speaker. It is important to emphasize that that clients do not have to believe the challenges at this point. The purpose here is to introduce the idea of questioning ATs rather than considering them established facts. This is typically a very brief segment that ends the session on a positive note.

Homework

The homework assignment at the end of chapter 5 is the first in a series of three assignments that lead up to fully integrated cognitive restructuring and self-paced exposure using Worksheet 7.1 (Be Your Own Cognitive Therapist (BYOCT) Worksheet). This time clients are asked to use Worksheet 5.2 (Monitoring Your Automatic Thoughts) to monitor their ATs and the emotions they cause in one to two naturally occurring situations during the week. The worksheet also asks clients to rate their belief in the ATs on a 0–100 scale, higher numbers indicating more confidence in the veracity of the AT. For now this rating is simply practice. Later, it can be used to help see the effectiveness of client's cognitive restructuring work. Be sure to inform the client that if no situations arise, he should imagine an anxiety-provoking situation and do the recording. These ATs will be used in the subsequent exercises.

Solutions to Common Difficulties

Client Is Unable to Identify ATs

Occasionally clients continue to have difficulty identifying their thoughts. If so, the therapist should take some time in session to review an extra situation or two to practice eliciting thoughts. The client can be encouraged to consider what someone else might think in that situation or what he is afraid might happen. As a last resort, the therapist can suggest what other socially anxious clients have thought in similar situations to see if it fits for this client. The client may be able to describe an image of the situation and that can be translated into verbal statements. To get started, it might be helpful to record everything on the board including emotions, positive thoughts, behaviors, and physiological reactions, with the hope that some ATs will be in the mix or can be derived from the other reactions. For example, "I felt myself starting to blush" might lead to the AT "She'll see I'm blushing." The reason that someone seeing the client blushing might be a problem may then be explored, and other ATs may arise from that discussion.

If by the end of the first few in-session exposures the client continues to have difficulty with the cognitive aspects of the treatment, cognitive restructuring activities can be simplified and greater emphasis placed on exposure. It is relatively rare for clients to be unable to identify some ATs once they are in the actual situations.

Client Is Unable to Identify Emotions

Emotion-focusing skills should be used to assist clients who have difficulty identifying their emotions. Here is an example of how that might be done:

Therapist: We wrote on the board that one of the ATs you have when you try to talk with managers or other people above you at work social events was that they would not want to talk to you. Do you remember how you felt when you have had that thought in those situations?

Client: Not really. I'm not a very optimistic person so I often think things like that.

Therapist: OK. Let's try to connect that AT a little bit more to any feelings you might experience. Sit for a moment and imagine yourself at that last holiday party you have described to me and think "That manager doesn't want to talk to me," and then try to pay attention to how it makes you feel.

Client: (*After a brief pause*) I guess it is kind of frustrating.

Therapist: You are feeling frustrated.

Client: Yes, frustrated because I know I am a good employee but I will never get ahead because I come off like such an idiot when I get scared in these situations.

Therapist: It sounds like maybe you are feeling frustrated because it seems like your social anxiety is holding you back professionally and maybe a little discouraged about whether that can change.

Client: Yes, I have tried so hard to be more social but maybe I was just born shy.

Therapist: That is helpful. You were able to identify three feelings that come from the AT, "That manager doesn't want to talk to me"—frustrated, scared, and discouraged. Paying attention to those feelings can be difficult at first but it is helpful because acknowledging the feelings sometimes leads us to other very important ATs.

Therapists trained in non-CBT approaches may be tempted to further explore the client's potentially rigid self-concept or shy personality. That would not be appropriate at this point because the goal is to teach the client the first steps in cognitive restructuring. Although such characterological attributions may be affectively laden and important, exploration of them may not be essential to overcoming social anxiety. As the client starts to see progress, this issue is likely to take care of itself. Once he has the skills in place, then the more in-depth exploration can occur for a central issue, typically in the context of an exposure. The client will then be in the position to truly benefit from the time and effort.

Additional Practice in Eliciting ATs

If the therapist believes a client could use additional practice in the first two steps of the cognitive restructuring process, then additional vignettes could be introduced. Any commonly encountered situation can work as practice. The client can either describe what ATs he would have, if the situation is relevant to him, or can imagine what someone might think in that situation. Some suggested vignettes are:

- Making a toast at a wedding

- Starting a conversation with a complete stranger at a party

- Starting a conversation while standing in line somewhere (e.g., a store, bank, health club, Department of Motor Vehicles)

- Running into an acquaintance one has not seen for a long time

- Asking a stranger for directions

- Returning an item to a store without the receipt

Chapter 10 | *Cognitive Restructuring: Challenging Automatic Thoughts*

(Corresponds to chapter 6 of the workbook)

Timeline

Typically one to two sessions

Materials Needed

- Copy of client workbook

- Dry erase board

- Social Anxiety Session Change Index (SASCI)

- Weekly Social Anxiety Session Change Graph (same copy as used last session)

- Table 5.1 (List of Thinking Errors)

- Figure 6.1 (Disputing Questions)

- Worksheet 6.1 (Practice Using Anxious Self/Coping Self Dialogue)

- Worksheet 6.2 (Cognitive Restructuring Practice)

Session Outline

- Review, score, and graph SASCI

- Review homework

- Challenge automatic thoughts

- Use rational responses

- Assign homework

- Prepare for first exposure session, if exposures will begin the following session

Homework

- Have the client complete Worksheet 6.2 (Cognitive Restructuring Practice).

- Instruct the client to read chapter 7 of the workbook, if exposures will begin the following session.

Overview

Chapter 6 of the workbook covers the remaining steps in cognitive restructuring. It builds on the first two steps, the identification of automatic thoughts (ATs) and the emotions they cause and identification of thinking errors, developed in chapter 5. As in chapter 5, the session opens with a review of the SASCI and homework. Then each concept is covered, first with neutral vignettes and then by application to the client's own experience. Homework for the upcoming week involves applying all of the cognitive restructuring skills to a naturally occurring situation. There is also a brief discussion in anticipation of the first exposure in the next session.

SASCI and Homework Review

Begin the session by administering the SASCI and graphing the score on the client's Weekly Social Anxiety Session Change Graph.

Most clients should be into the routine of completing homework each week by now. If the homework was completed, detailed review of the assignment to monitor and label ATs (Worksheet 5.2—Monitoring Your

Automatic Thoughts) can be delayed, as this information is used extensively in session. The therapist should acknowledge completion and that the material will be used throughout the session, however.

If the client did not complete Worksheet 5.2, she should be asked to complete it at the beginning of the session because the material is used extensively in teaching the remaining steps of cognitive restructuring. Only three or four ATs are needed for the subsequent work. If homework compliance is an ongoing problem, review the strategies in chapter 4 of this therapist guide to improve homework success. In the next week or two, homework will begin to involve *in vivo* therapeutic exposures and those are unlikely to be completed if less threatening self-monitoring has not been done. Homework compliance is so important that it may be worth delaying the start of exposures a week or two for additional practice with the cognitive skills with in-session time spent on problem-solving or cognitive restructuring about the importance of homework if compliance is still poor (e.g., homework rarely attempted). Completing the reading of the next assigned chapter is also important but this is more about efficiency as the therapist can cover the material in session.

Step 3 of Cognitive Restructuring: Disputing Questions

The last session covered the first two steps of cognitive restructuring, identifying ATs and the emotions they cause and identifying thinking errors. Once the client has a rudimentary understanding of thinking errors, then the therapist should move on to Step 3 of cognitive restructuring—challenging the ATs using disputing questions. The primary skill to be taught involves placing the AT in a relevant blank space on the list of disputing questions found in the workbook (Figure 6.1) and then answering the question. After a brief explanation, the therapist guides the client in practicing on ATs from the vignette for which ATs were previously categorized. The AT is the "Anxious Voice" (Anxious Beth in the vignette in the client workbook) and the disputing question is the "Coping Voice" (Coping Beth). Once the client has the basic concept, further practice should use the ATs from the client's homework using the Anxious Self/Coping Self Dialogue (Worksheet 6.1).

The disputing questions are only a starting point. There are many other useful questions that could be asked for a given situation or thought. The therapist should not hesitate to deviate from this list. On the other hand, it is helpful to use the disputing questions initially, as these are the only source the client has available when practicing the cognitive restructuring skills on her own, and it is unlikely that the client will generate many alternative disputing questions at this early point.

The biggest mistake that therapists make in this step of cognitive restructuring is failing to have the client answer the disputing question. Often this is because the answer seems obvious to the therapist. For example, "Do I know for certain that I will not have anything to say?" may become an example of therapist mind-reading. Because no one can predict the future accurately, the obvious answer is "No, I don't know for *certain*." However, the obvious answer to the client may be "Yes, I've been in that situation many times, and it always goes badly." By getting the answer to the question, the therapist can either challenge the certainty of the outcome ("Are you *100%* certain?"), the certainty the pattern will be repeated ("Does running out of things to say last time have to equal running out of things to say in this conversation?"), or the extent of the problem ("What evidence do you have that you will not have *anything* to say?").

Another problematic pattern occurs when the therapist poses a series of disputing questions to which the client responds with a series of ATs. For example, a client has identified the AT, "Everyone will see how anxious I am." The therapist then poses a disputing question such as "Do you have any evidence that some people might not even notice that you are blushing?" to which the client responds "People have commented on my blushing in the past so I know that my blushing is really obvious to everyone." The therapist may then pose another disputing question such as "Do you know for certain that your blushing is obvious to everyone?" to which the client responds "I don't see how anyone could miss it," and so on. It is not uncommon for this type of interaction pattern to leave both the client and the therapist feeling frustrated and misunderstood. There are several approaches to dealing with this problematic pattern. One is for the therapist to make sure that the client is the one posing the disputing questions. Clients often give less defensive answers when they question their own thoughts than when they respond to the same question posed by the therapist. Letting the client take the lead in questioning can be quite difficult for novice therapists who are eager to help clients change their thinking but impatient with clients who struggle to find ways to question their ATs when possible avenues of questioning seem so obvious to the therapist. Additionally, it may be helpful if the therapist explicitly labels the distorted answer as an AT and not the realistic alternative to the original AT that the disputing question was intended to elicit. In the example just presented, the therapist might respond to the client's first answer by saying:

> *That's an important new AT. Let me add it to our list. "My blushing is really obvious because people have commented on it in the past." OK, now let's go back to the original thought "Everyone will see how anxious I am." Remember, the goal of the disputing questions is to practice taking an alternative perspective that is hopefully more realistic and less anxiety-provoking. Which disputing question on the list might help you to do that? It's also OK if you don't believe your answer to the disputing question 100% at this point.*

In our experience using this portion of the client workbook, we have found that clients often do not recognize that their responses to the disputing questions contain ATs. Clients can move through the Anxious Self/Coping Self dialogues quickly without really exploring the answers and following up with additional disputing questions. Instead they tend to move on to the next AT from the original list. It is helpful to slow down the process in session and have clients really consider their answers and see if they are helpful or productive. In the workbook, this is described as ATs that might be "hiding out underneath" other ATs, a process familiar to experienced therapists but often novel to clients.

Also the therapist should keep in mind that the Anxious Self/Coping Self dialogue format is a useful intermediate tool for learning these skills. Soon, for many clients by the next session or two, they can move away from this structure and use a more flexible process of exploring ATs and disputing questions and answers in a dynamic fashion. Note that in subsequent sessions in the workbook, this explicit format fades away.

Typically, two to four different challenges to each of four to five ATs are sufficient practice. Although the goal is to learn the skill, not necessarily to change the client's ATs, very often clients have a positive reaction to the exercise. As they see that their thinking is dysfunctional and begin to consider other points of view, the powerful effect of changing their thinking becomes a reality.

As with work on thinking errors, this material is most effective if the therapist is thoroughly familiar with the procedures. It is often helpful to anticipate the ATs likely to be reported by a client and rehearse using various disputing questions as challenges.

Step 4 of Cognitive Restructuring: Generating Rational Responses

Generating rational responses is the most difficult step for clients and novice therapists to learn. The goal is to come up with a phrase or statement that summarizes the most important point(s) made when challenging an AT with disputing questions. At this point (and probably through the first couple of in-session exposures), the therapist may have to offer suggestions for rational responses. Ideally, the therapist and the client summarize the points made in the earlier cognitive restructuring, and this pulls the concepts together sufficiently for the client to generate a rational response. For example, using the situation of Beth and her upcoming job interview in the workbook, the therapist might say, "So you have made several important points here. You said that you would like to make a good first impression but you might be able to make up for it if you don't. They already have a good impression of you from your resume because they invited you to interview. You have more than the minimum required experience for the job. Can you summarize those points into a rational response that will remind you of them when you are feeling anxious about the interview?" If that support is insufficient, the therapist can then offer an idea and assist the client in putting it into her own words. Continuing with the same example, the therapist might say, "How about something about already having made a good enough impression with your resume to get the interview?" If the client continues to struggle, the therapist can simply make a couple of suggestions and let the client choose which one fits best. "How about 'I'm qualified for this job' or 'They liked me enough to interview me.'" Clients and therapists should not hesitate to use the suggested rational responses from page 114 of the workbook, summarized in Table 10.1 here.

Table 10.1 Commonly Used Rational Responses

Looking for nonequivalence

_____ $\neq$ _____

The first blank is something you are worried about such as looking nervous, being rejected, experiencing an anxiety symptom, and so forth. The second blank is an outcome you are worried about such as not getting something you want. Some examples are:

Look nervous $\neq$ looking foolish
Being rejected $\neq$ being alone forever
Not getting this job $\neq$ never getting a good job
Blushing $\neq$ looking stupid
Feeling anxious $\neq$ looking anxious

The worst that can happen . . .

The worst that can happen is_____ and I can live with that.
The worst that can happen is_____, but that is unlikely.

Setting attainable goals as Rational Responses

I only have to say hello.
I only have to make it through the first couple of minutes and then I'll be OK.

I just need to get three points across.

Homework

Homework for chapter 6 of the client workbook is the next step toward use of Worksheet 7.1 (Be Your Own Cognitive Therapist (BYOCT)), which is introduced in chapter 7 of the workbook. Worksheet 6.2 (Cognitive Restructuring Practice) again asks the client to monitor a naturally occurring situation during the week, followed by going through all four steps of cognitive restructuring. This will be the first opportunity for clients to try the entire cognitive restructuring procedure on their own. The Anxious Self/Coping Self Dialogue will help with challenging the ATs. This format will be faded out in the next iteration of this worksheet as clients gain more confidence with the skills and can benefit from greater flexibility. As with the last homework form, Worksheet 6.2 asks clients to rate their belief in the ATs on the 0–100 scale. A similar belief rating is made for the rational response. These ratings help the client and the therapist see how emotionally invested the client is in the ATs and rational response. At this point, it is acceptable if the belief ratings are high for the ATs and low for the rational response. This should change once the client has some success in exposures.

This is a fairly challenging homework assignment, so it is helpful to encourage clients to refer to chapters 5 and 6 as well as the sample completed worksheet shown in Figure 6.1. As usual, if no anxiety-provoking situations arise before the next session, an imaginal scene can be used.

Anticipation of the First Exposure

The first in-session exposure is a key moment in this treatment. For the first time, all of the therapeutic elements come together. However, the exposure is an unfamiliar situation with unknown expectations that may elicit significant anticipatory anxiety. Therefore, the therapist needs to exercise both caution and decisiveness when initiating the first exposure.

If the client has a reasonable grasp of the cognitive restructuring procedures, then it is time to go onto the first exposure. (A "reasonable grasp" is defined as being able to move from one step to the next with cues from the therapist and understanding that the purpose is to consider alternative points of view about ATs.) The first exposure requires more time than the typical session provides, and we recommend that an extended 90-min session be scheduled. If there is extra time in the session devoted to the material in chapter 6 of the workbook, then the therapist should initiate additional practice with the cognitive restructuring rather than trying to start the next chapter. If the client continues to have difficulty generating ATs and does not seem to grasp the steps of cognitive restructuring, then it is preferable to spend an additional session developing these skills. The therapist and the client can identify additional anxiety-provoking situations and work through the cognitive restructuring practice. The homework in chapter 6 can be repeated to give additional practice between sessions.

Once the therapist decides to initiate an in-session exposure, the client and the therapist should briefly review what exposure entails at the end of the immediately preceding session. The goal is to inform the client so that she will not be surprised or frightened into avoidance. It is helpful to explicitly acknowledge that clients are likely to have some anticipatory anxiety during the upcoming week but that starting exposure means they are progressing as expected through treatment. It is time to start applying some of the new skills. However, because the client may be quite anxious and wish to escape the situation, it is important to maintain maximum flexibility about the specific situation that will be the focus of the exposure, so no specific topics or situations should be promised at this time. Remind clients that exposure is graduated and will start with a situation that they can handle. Furthermore, the situation will ultimately be determined in a negotiation between the client and the therapist.

We also always mention that the client may have the inclination to avoid the next session. By explicitly discussing this possibility, the client realizes that any cancellation due to illness or an emergency will be treated with some skepticism. Of course, actual session conflicts arise, but rarely. Anticipation of the first exposure is a perfect opportunity to practice the cognitive restructuring skills. This can either be done within the session (for clients who are extremely concerned) or as an additional practice between sessions (for most clients). The bottom line is that the therapist wants to communicate that anticipation of the first exposure is an anxiety-provoking situation but he or she believes the client is fully capable of coping with that anxiety. The therapist should never communicate that anxiety is to be avoided. The therapist's verbal and nonverbal communication should clearly indicate his or her empathy and understanding that this is an anxiety-provoking event but, more importantly, that this is a routine next step that the client is prepared to handle. An extended empathic exploration of the client's anxiety will only increase it. A practical focus on using the cognitive restructuring skills to manage the anxiety and committing to approach rather than avoidance is most productive.

Solutions to Common Difficulties

Client Is Unable to Report ATs or Only Reports the Same Ones

In a few cases, the client gets to this point in therapy and continues to have difficulty identifying ATs or always reports the same one or two thoughts (e.g., "I'll get anxious"). As discussed in chapter 9, efforts can be made to infer what the ATs might be or to infer the implications of the few ATs the client reports. At this point, the best option is to use the exposure as a vehicle for the generation of additional ATs. Sometimes the immediacy of the situation makes it easier for clients to identify their thoughts. If that does not work, then the cognitive aspects of the treatment can be de-emphasized, as will be discussed in chapter 12 of this therapist guide.

Client Fails to Grasp Basic Cognitive Restructuring Skills

Clients are quite variable in the rate at which they develop cognitive restructuring skills. Some clients grasp the notion of logical analysis very quickly and are eager to apply it in actual situations. Others have more difficulty for a variety of reasons. It is sometimes helpful to spend an extra session practicing the four steps of cognitive restructuring on situations relevant to the client's presenting problems. If the client continues to struggle after extra practice, then it is time to consider possible causes for the difficulty.

Clients with limited education or intellectual capacity may not make the logical connections that underlie cognitive restructuring quickly or easily. In such cases, it is often sufficient to simplify the procedures as follows: (a) focus on one simple AT at a time, pick only one possible thinking error, use short, simple questions for challenging the AT, and have the therapist supply the rational response; (b) attempt to develop a rational response that applies to many situations and encourage the client to use it routinely; (c) if the identification of thinking errors is problematic, reduce the list to only the two to three most common ones for the client or eliminate this step altogether; and (d) write more notes on the board so the client both hears and reads the material.

Occasionally clients are so anxious in the session that they have difficulty using the cognitive restructuring skills. In such cases, the work they do for homework is often quite good, so it is clear they can utilize the procedures. As the client becomes more comfortable in session, the problem often takes care of itself. The therapist can facilitate the client comfort by being highly supportive, acknowledging the anxiety, and avoiding triggering fears of negative evaluation. In particular, long pauses while awaiting a client's response are rarely productive for highly anxious clients. Sometimes it is helpful to try to apply the cognitive restructuring skills to the situation of coming to session. Explicitly discussing the client's anxiety in session frees her from having to hide it from the therapist. Also, the therapist can then acknowledge greater comfort with repeated exposure to therapy sessions as it becomes apparent.

Cognitive restructuring is a very Western, analytical mode of thinking. Most people who function in Western cultures should be able to utilize the logical analyses that come easily to therapists with Western educations. However, therapists should be very sensitive to clients' own thinking styles and belief systems. Certain outcomes or interpretations of interpersonal behavior may be culturally specific but seem illogical to a therapist who does not share the same cultural background. For example, the acceptability of highly assertive behavior varies by culture and gender, making a client's AT that such behavior will lead to rejection more or less valid. Also, some people think more in a gestalt or nonverbal manner that makes detailed analyses of the specific meanings of words or probabilities somewhat foreign to them. For example, on page 180 of the client workbook, we break the possible meanings of a client's hand shaking into nine probability segments of a pie chart. With a less analytical thinker, we might simply draw a balance scale on the board and "stack" the possible meanings on the positive or negative end to create an overall sense of the "weight" of the evidence. The overall sense of balance derived from this strategy will appeal to some clients for whom the notion of conditional probabilities is incomprehensible.

When considering personal style and culture, the therapist must engage in a careful balancing act of encouraging the client to utilize new skills yet keeping those skills in a familiar context that draws upon the client's strengths. After all, if the client's own resources were sufficient, she would not be seeking treatment. On the other hand, coping techniques that are entirely dissonant with the client's worldview are unlikely to be utilized over the long term. In such cases a blend may be the best option. For example, with a highly religious client one might use the following rational response for a fear of starting conversations: "I'll say hello and one more thing, then trust God not to let me get into a situation He and I can't handle together." This response includes a standard cognitive-behavioral therapy coping strategy—setting a reasonable goal. However, it also draws upon the client's spiritual beliefs to emphasize that the anxiety will not spiral out of control.

Client Has Difficulty Developing a Rational Response

As noted previously, this is often the most difficult step of the cognitive restructuring procedures, for clients and for beginning therapists. Often in the first several iterations of the procedure in session and as homework, the client will need substantial support finding a rational response. In session, the therapist may end up suggesting the rational response, helping the client put it into her own words. For homework, the client may simply draw from some of the suggestions in the book or one that was used previously. The therapist can support the client's efforts by summarizing the answers to the disputing questions in a way that starts to imply potential rational responses. It may also be helpful to write the answers to the disputing questions on the board in session or on paper for the BYOCT homework. Rather than trying to design a short catchy phrase immediately, longer summaries of the disputing questions' answers can often be massaged into a core idea that is a good short rational response.

Chapter 11 | *Exposure and Cognitive Restructuring: First Exposure*

(Corresponds to chapter 7 of the workbook)

Timeline

Should be one session, but may be an extended session up to 90 min

Materials Needed

■ Copy of client workbook

■ Dry erase board

■ Social Anxiety Session Change Index (SASCI)

■ Weekly Social Anxiety Session Change Graph (same copy as used last session)

■ Table 5.1 (List of Thinking Errors)

■ Figure 6.1 (Disputing Questions)

■ Form for Recording Key Information During In-Session Exposures That Can Serve as Session Progress Note

■ Worksheet 7.1 (Be Your Own Cognitive Therapist (BYOCT) Worksheet)

Therapist Note

■ *You will need approximately 20 copies of Worksheet 7.1 and 6–10 copies of the recording form for the duration of treatment.* ■

Session Outline

- Review, score, and graph SASCI

- Review homework

- Briefly review rationale for systematic graduated exposure

- Complete first in-session exposure, including:
    Identifying the situation

    Cognitive restructuring

    Setting a behavioral goal

    The exposure itself
- Debrief the exposure

- Assign homework

Homework

- Have the client complete exposure homework including Worksheet 7.1 (Be Your Own Cognitive Therapist (BYOCT) Worksheet).

- Instruct the client to read chapter 8 of the workbook; one of chapters 9, 10, or 11 may also be assigned at this time.

Therapist Note

It is likely that the session in which the first exposure is conducted will run over 1 hr. It is important to briefly review the rationale for exposure and then to carefully go through the whole process of doing an exposure: plan, preprocess, do the exposure, and postprocess. Also, you will need to plan the first out-of-session exposure and the next in-session exposure. Therefore, it is a good idea to set aside 1.5 hr for this session.

Overview

As usual, the session should start with a quick review of the SASCI and homework from the previous session. The therapist should take care that the client does not try to extend this discussion as an avoidance of the upcoming exposure.

The first in-session exposure is a highlight of this therapy. It is the first opportunity to fully integrate all of the therapeutic elements. Everything up to this point has been preparation for facing feared situations. The first exposure session can be challenging for both the therapist and the client. Done well, however, it is highly energizing. Experienced therapists typically enjoy the challenge of exposures, perhaps because fairly rapid client progress often results. All of the information needed to conduct a successful first exposure is included in chapter 7 of the workbook. Here we will highlight some of the key points and add additional pointers.

Timing of the First Exposure

In our research protocols for individual therapy, we specify that exposure must occur no later than session eight of treatment. As noted, it is time to do exposure if the client has a reasonable grasp of the cognitive restructuring skills. Few clients will be truly proficient in cognitive restructuring, but their skills develop rapidly once they start using the techniques in exposures. By this point, the client should also be reasonably comfortable in session, although anxiety will likely spike for the first exposure session. The therapeutic alliance should be sufficiently developed that the client is able to trust the therapist to engage in exposure. The therapist should know enough about the client's fears to develop an exposure scenario that is appropriately challenging.

Picking the First Exposure Situation

Pages 127–138 of the workbook contain detailed information about appropriate situations for the first exposure that should be reviewed in preparation for the first exposure session. Prior to the session, the therapist should review the client's Fear and Avoidance Hierarchy and determine what situation will likely be role-played. As noted in the workbook, a situation with a Subjective Units of Discomfort Scale

(SUDS) rating of 40–50 on the hierarchy is about the right place to start. If in doubt, go to a slightly less anxiety-provoking situation. The client may not perceive exposure to situations that are too easy as an accomplishment, however. Thought should be given to any needed props or rearrangement of the furniture to help with staging.

With the vast majority of clients, we use one of two situations for the first exposure. For clients with fears of interacting with others, we stage a casual conversation that requires little specialty knowledge for the therapist role player. For individuals primarily seeking treatment for public speaking fears, we have them sit and tell about a recent experience as if telling a story in a casual group. Usually one of these two scenarios can be adapted for clients with other primary feared situations.

For the first exposure, simple, straightforward scenarios that require little "pretending" are the best. Save complex situations or ones that require the role player to take on the role of a specific person for later sessions. Also, the situation needs to be flexible so the length can vary to adjust for the client's anxiety level. Situations with specific endpoints, such as making a request, work less well for the first exposure.

Integrating Exposure and Cognitive Restructuring

Therapists inexperienced with this treatment often try to do too much cognitive restructuring prior to the first exposure. The goal is to show the client how the cognitive restructuring can be used when facing feared situations and perhaps offer some initial help with a superficial automatic thought (AT). In-depth cognitive work will come later. Most likely the client is too anxious to engage in it now anyway.

If the client is proficient at identifying ATs, then up to five or six may be recorded on the board. However, two to three are sufficient. The therapist should pick one (at most two) AT(s) to pursue for cognitive restructuring, being sure to touch briefly on the emotions elicited by the ATs. Focus on ATs that have a behavioral element, if possible. Good choices are "I'll run out of things to say," "I won't know what to say," or "I'll look stupid/incompetent/foolish." Avoid thoughts that reflect core beliefs about acceptability as a person or the need to be perfect or that relate to past bad experiences. Have the client rate his belief in the target AT on the 0–100 scale.

One or two thinking errors can be considered for the target AT, followed by challenges with the disputing questions. Typically the challenges can end when the client is able to consider that there is more than one possible outcome. Clients who have fears about what to say typically reach this point when they are able to generate a list of possible topics. These topics should be recorded on the board for reference during the role play.

Although it is easy to skip setting an achievable behavioral goal to save time, this step is essential. Despite the high anxiety typically evoked by anticipation of the first exposure, clients are very likely to discount the experience afterward or believe they failed miserably because they became anxious. The goal provides a mutually agreed-upon benchmark against which to evaluate the experience. Clients who discount the experience can be reminded they were not confident the goal was achievable prior to the exposure. Clients who believe they failed by becoming anxious can be reminded that lack of anxiety was not the goal. Very often the dual goal set for the first exposure is "Stay in the situation until the therapist stops the role play" and "Use the rational response to help manage anxiety." The therapist can control these outcomes by stopping the exposure when the client is actively engaged in the role play and by prompting the client to repeat the rational response when taking SUDS ratings, which should occur approximately every minute of the exposure. For the first exposure, therapists should be 100% confident the goal can be achieved, even if it requires some manipulation of the situation on the part of the therapist.

Debriefing the Exposure

Debriefing the exposure is often the most powerful portion of the intervention for several reasons. Both the client and the therapist can provide a perspective on the actual experience. The elicitation of the client's affect indicates that the relevant schema is fully engaged. The most difficult portion of the session is over, so the client has the cognitive capacity to engage in processing the experience. All of these factors work to the therapist's advantage to facilitate a productive interaction. *This advantage is lost if the therapist manages time poorly and has to short-change the postexposure debriefing.*

Review of Behavioral Goal

Clients and therapists typically have very different views of what occurred during the exposure. Therefore, it is essential that the therapist first listen carefully to the client's perspective before offering any opinions. The therapist should explore the client's point of view on goal attainment and what went well or poorly in the exposure. The therapist can use the cognitive restructuring model to explore the client's evidence for poor performance or outcomes. Any mention of success should be explicitly noted, as clients are rarely able to give themselves credit for success. After the client has provided his perspective on the role play, the therapist's perspective on goal attainment and how well the exposure went may be given. In later exposures, outside role players may also be asked to share their reactions with the client and answer any questions the client has about what they thought of the exposure.

The most helpful feedback from the therapist and other exposure participants emphasizes information counter to the client's negative beliefs. For example, a client whose first exposure was a conversation may have become highly anxious, asked the therapist/role player only one question, and otherwise simply responded to questions. In this situation, the therapist might emphasize the many things the client feared would happen but which did not actually come to pass (e.g., he would have several long pauses, be too anxious to think of anything to say, look foolish, etc.). Additionally, only in rare cases do clients look as anxious as they think they do (see chapter 2), so it is often quite appropriate to acknowledge that the client showed some symptoms of anxiety (e.g., blushed, stumbled over words) but, at the same time, to point out that it did not detract from enjoyment of the conversation, seemed to decrease over time, and so on. Therapists who deny seeing any anxiety in a client who was obviously anxious risk damaging their credibility.

Review of the SUDS Pattern

Typically, the pattern of SUDS ratings during the exposure is quickly graphed for the client, with SUDS on the Y axis and time on the X axis. Different patterns of SUDS can be used to make different points. A common pattern is for the initial SUDS ratings to be rather high and then to decline over time. In these cases, the therapist can point out that it seems like getting started is the hardest part and that if the client hangs in there, things seem to get easier. The therapist and the client would then watch for this pattern over the course of several exposures and, if appropriate, develop a new rational response (e.g., "It gets easier"; "The hardest part is getting started").

Several points may be discussed for clients with high SUDS ratings that show no decline over time. If the client still met his goals (e.g., shared an opinion during the speech and answered a question), it can be pointed out that a person can simultaneously be quite anxious and still do what he needs to do in a given social situation. A rational response arising from this observation may be "I can be anxious and still give a reasonable talk." It is also helpful to inquire about ATs that may have interfered with habituation so that they might be addressed in the next exposure.

Another common pattern is for the client to report either decreasing or steady SUDS ratings that spike when the client perceives a difficulty arising during the exposure. Sometimes the therapist will be able to figure out through observation what led to the spike in anxiety (e.g., there was a pause in the conversation, the client lost his place during a speech, etc.). At other times, it may not be as obvious. In either case, it is recommended that a note be made about what is happening during the exposure at the time of the increase in SUDS ratings (using the recording form provided at the end of this chapter). The therapist should ask the client what he was thinking at that point in the exposure (e.g., "Pauses reflect my incompetence," "The audience is getting impatient"). Such discussions may lead to new goals (e.g., "Allow yourself to pause twice during the conversation so that you can learn not to fear it") and targets for cognitive restructuring in the moment as well as during future exposures (i.e., the belief that pauses reflect incompetence). They also reinforce the relationship between thoughts and emotions.

Examination of the Evidence and Re-rating Belief in AT and Rational Response

After the exposure the therapist should ask the client to examine the evidence both for and against the target AT and the rational response, using disputing questions, feedback from exposure participants, and any other available information. The client should then be asked to re-rate his belief in both AT and rational response on the 0–100 scale. Ideally, evidence gained from the exposure will decrease belief in the AT and increase confidence in the rational response. Notable changes can be explored further to help both the client and the therapist understand what aspect of the exposure and cognitive work was helpful in the cognitive change. A lack of change on the ratings may also be explored to determine where the cognitive work or exposure were not as helpful as they could be, perhaps providing information to guide the planning of homework assignments or later in-session exposures.

Ending with a Take-Home Message

Debriefing of an exposure always ends with a challenge to the client to summarize what was learned in the experience that can be used later. The formulation of this take-home message forces one additional trial of processing schema-discrepant information. It also serves as a good source of evidence for later cognitive restructuring. Very often the summary for the first exposure reflects that it was not as difficult as the client expected or that he was able to stay in the situation despite high anxiety. The therapist should also make a mental note of anything that can be used as evidence for future cognitive restructuring (e.g., the client's ability to carry on a conversation can be used to challenge ATs about poor conversation skills).

Duration of Exposure

Most in-session exposures last between 5 min and 10 min. The first exposure may be shorter if the client is extremely anxious. The therapist, not the client, should control when the exposure ends. This is partially done by establishing scenarios that do not have a definite endpoint. It is best to stop when things are going fairly smoothly so the client perceives that he could have continued longer rather than being "saved by the bell."

Ideally, the client's SUDS ratings increase to greater than 60–70 and then start to decrease. If the SUDS ratings do not go this high, that is acceptable. Do not continue the exposure indefinitely in the hope that the anxiety will decrease. If possible, do not stop the exposure when the SUDS ratings are increasing, as this reinforces escape behavior when the anxiety peaks. Also, the client loses the opportunity to learn that the anxiety will decrease eventually. It is acceptable to stop the exposure when the anxiety has plateaued for two to three ratings on the assumption it would eventually come down. If the therapist perceives that the client has had a successful experience in the exposure and continuation risks a decrement in performance, the therapist may look for evidence that the client is slightly less anxious, take a SUDS rating, and end the exposure. This allows the exposure to end on a positive note.

Solutions to Common Difficulties

There are a couple of common difficulties inexperienced therapists encounter when conducting the first exposure.

Not Getting a Role Play Done

Once the decision is made to do an exposure, it needs to take place during that session. To do otherwise is extremely unfair to the client. The client is likely to be highly anxious, and he will be even more anxious if another week elapses before the first exposure. The need to get the first exposure done is one reason why we recommend not being too detailed in the previous week about the exposure situation. If necessary, the role play can be simple, not too anxiety-provoking, and brief (2–3 min). The important thing is to be able to celebrate the success of facing the first exposure. The alternative is facilitating avoidance behavior and communicating that the client may not be ready to face his fears.

To a large extent, the exposure gets done because the momentum carries the client and the therapist along. Therapists should never introduce an exposure by asking if the client wants to do it. In an effort to be supportive, inexperienced therapists may introduce the exposure by saying "What do you think about working on having conversations with strangers today?" This opens up the opportunity for the client to negotiate the situation and/or the need to do exposure at all. It is better to state "Today we will start working directly on your fears about having conversations with strangers. As you think about that situation, what ATs come to mind?" Then the therapist has moved directly into cognitive restructuring and any fears the client has about the exposure can be handled within that context. If it turns out the client is extremely anxious and is barely able to stay in the room for the exposure, the therapist has the flexibility to make the exposure easy and short without communicating that the client has failed to complete some higher standard originally set by the therapist.

Time Management

There is a lot of material to cover in the first exposure session. Both the client and the therapist may be anxious and tend to spend extra time on familiar ground before proceeding to the exposure. Therefore, it is essential to keep the session on track, and it is a good idea to budget extra time for the initial exposure session. Up to 1.5 hr may be scheduled for this appointment. Nevertheless, it is essential to keep the session on track. We strongly recommend the following timeline for this session:

Min 0–10: Greetings, SASCI, homework review

Min 10–15: Remind the client this is the first exposure, briefly review the rationale for exposure, and describe the situation to be role-played

Min 15–30: Cognitive restructuring steps 1–4

Min 30–40: Elaborate the role-play scenario and set an achievable behavioral goal

Min 40–50: Complete role play

Min 50–75: Debrief exposure

Min 75–90: Negotiate homework

The client's anxiety about the new procedures and upcoming role play is usually so high that in-depth cognitive restructuring cannot be done. Therefore, it is best to pick one straightforward ATs and move through the steps fairly rapidly. More time can be spent on the cognitive restructuring during the debriefing because the client will be less anxious and more able to engage in the process. Also, the role-play experience may generate key ATs or provide evidence to challenge the ones identified previously.

Overall, the best therapeutic strategy to manage the client's anxiety is to be highly supportive but move the session along so the feared experience is over in a reasonable period of time. This may mean that the therapist provides more direction than will be appropriate later, including suggesting thinking errors, a rational response, and an achievable behavioral goal. Usually the therapist explicitly mentions that there is a lot to cover and it is best to move fairly quickly.

In future exposure sessions, the session timeline would look like this (for 60 min session, allow extra debriefing time):

Min 0–10: Greetings, SASCI, homework review

Min 10–25: Describe the situation to be role-played; cognitive restructuring steps 1–4

Min 25–35: Complete role play

Min 35–45: Debrief exposure

Min 45–50: Negotiate homework

It is quite easy to short-change the debriefing when time management problems arise, especially after returning to the format of a 50–60 min session for the remaining exposures. However, in addition to decreasing the probability that the client will get the full benefit of the exposure, research suggests that socially anxious individuals tend to engage in maladaptive postprocessing of anxiety-provoking social situations. Consequently, it is possible for a client who has not had a sufficient debriefing to walk away from a role play that the therapist perceived as quite successful and ruminate over the experience as a failure—leading to more anxiety about approaching similar situations in the future.

One of the challenges of in-session exposure in individual treatment is that the therapist must wear a number of hats at the same time. In the first exposure, and perhaps in later exposures, the therapist serves as the role-play partner or audience member. Thus, simultaneously the therapist is engaging in the role play, monitoring the client's experience, requesting and recording periodic SUDS ratings, watching for the attainment of goals, and timing the exposure. We have developed a few strategies to help make these multiple tasks more feasible.

The Form for Recording Key Information During In-Session Exposures That Can Serve as Session Progress Note provides space for recording details of the exposure, the goal, and SUDS ratings that we developed for research. Make copies of this form so it will be available for each exposure. Some details can be filled in after the session as the form can double as a progress note.

It is helpful to have a clock visible to the therapist during the role play. This prevents the therapist from needing to check a watch and potentially conveying boredom to the client during the role play.

The therapist should clearly distinguish between the therapist role and being a role player. This is most important if the role play involves a potentially awkward situation such as requesting a date or expressing positive or negative feelings. Overt behavioral cues help the client distinguish the roles. For example, we always have an extra chair in the room so the therapist never sits in his or her "therapist chair" when engaging in a role play. The therapist then switches back to the therapist chair for the debriefing. Standing for the role play, using props, or rearranging the furniture can also provide important behavioral cues.

Use of an easel with paper or white board greatly facilitates the exposure process. The therapist should write the ATs on the board and use the board for any illustrations that facilitate cognitive restructuring. For example, we often make lists of conversation topics as evidence to counter the common AT "I don't know what to say." In later chapters, there are examples of pie charts or other sketches that can facilitate cognitive restructuring. The Rational Response should also be written where it is visible to the client during the role play. An easel with paper has the advantage that the rational response can be recorded on a subsequent page, thus reducing the client's focus on his ATs during the exposure but without losing access to the ATs if needed in later cognitive restructuring.

What Counts as a Successful First Exposure

Both therapists and clients may have high expectations (and high anxiety) about the first exposure. It may be helpful for therapists to utilize the cognitive restructuring skills for themselves. A good goal for therapists inexperienced in this treatment is to simply get through all of the procedures. This is a demanding session. If the client's experience is positive enough that he is likely to return the following week, then the session is a success. Therapists who are more comfortable with the procedures are typically able to make useful progress on challenging ATs and fear reduction as well.

What to Do If the Exposure Fails

Prevention is the best antidote to failure. The therapist needs to take great care to set up the exposure so the client is carried along by the momentum and has little opportunity to engage in avoidance behavior. Clients may desire to avoid the anxiety evoked by exposure but they nearly always have a strong negative reaction when the therapist sets up circumstances that allow this to happen. It is up to the therapist to manipulate the details of the exposure so that the client can achieve success.

The therapist needs to listen very carefully to the client's experience of the role play during the debriefing. On rare occasions, a client will perceive a catastrophic failure and become very distressed, possibly not returning to therapy. This can be prevented if the therapist fully understands the client's perception of the experience rather than relying on his own judgment. The client's cognitions relating to his distress can be addressed through cognitive restructuring during the debriefing.

With the hundreds of socially anxious clients we have seen over the past 20 years, there has been only a small handful who have refused or escaped exposures. These are always the most severely impaired individuals who have great difficulty tolerating anxiety. In many cases, they are individuals who become angry when they perceive they will be unable to avoid an anxiety-provoking situation—the "fight" portion of the fight-or-flight response. If clients refuse or escape the first exposure, the therapist's top priority is to engage them. The therapist should explore what went wrong and develop a plan to proceed. This may include making exposure more gradual if the client can identify a situation he feels able to confront. Alternatively, the client may need further assistance in controlling anxiety symptoms. This could include medication or additional anxiety management procedures such as applied progressive muscle relaxation.

A client's failure to engage in exposure severely disrupts the therapeutic alliance. The therapist will need to put substantial effort into rebuilding rapport by communicating that the client did not fail therapy or disappoint the therapist. The therapist's willingness to continue to work with the client at the client's current level of functioning will help reestablish the alliance.

Homework

Typically homework after the first exposure includes an assignment for *in vivo* exposure, which is integrated with cognitive restructuring through the use of Worksheet 7.1 (BYOCT Worksheet). As a rule of thumb, pick something related to, but slightly less challenging than, the in-session exposure. Make sure the client fully agrees to do the assignment and that logistical obstacles are unlikely to arise. If necessary, make a backup plan. For example, the assignment might be to speak up twice at an upcoming meeting. If the meeting does not occur, the backup plan is to join coworkers at Friday afternoon happy hour and tell a brief story. As with all homework, it is important to write down the agreed-upon exposure so that there is no confusion later regarding what the task was and "forgetting" becomes a less probable explanation for not doing the *in vivo* exposure.

It is important to review Worksheet 7.1 during homework assignment. Highlight how this worksheet outlines the same procedures used in the session. Emphasize the need to do both the cognitive preparation before the self-initiated exposure (p. 1) and the debriefing after the exposure (p. 2).

Form for Recording Key Information During In-Session Exposures That Can Serve as Session Progress Note

Client Name	Date
Description of Exposure	
Primary AT	
Rational Response	
Observable Behavioral Goal	
Role player(s)	

SUDS Ratings	Progress Note
1.	
2.	
3.	
4.	
5.	
6.	
7.	
8.	
9.	
10.	

Chapter 12 *Exposure and Cognitive Restructuring: Ongoing Exposure*

(Corresponds to chapter 8 of the workbook)

Timeline

Typically five to six sessions in the recommended 16-session treatment program, but can vary up to 10 sessions or more if the client is making good progress but needs more in-sessions exposures)

Materials Needed

- Copy of client workbook

- Dry erase board

- Social Anxiety Session Change Index (SASCI)

- Weekly Social Anxiety Session Change Graph (same copy as used last session)

- Table 5.1 (List of Thinking Errors)

- Figure 6.1 (Disputing Questions)

- Form for Recording Key Information During In-Session Exposures That Can Serve as Session Progress Note

- Worksheet 7.1 (Be Your Own Cognitive Therapist (BYOCT) Worksheet)

Session Outline

- Review, score, and graph SASCI

- Review homework

- Complete cognitive restructuring and exposure

- Assign homework

Homework

- Have the client complete exposure homework including Worksheet 7.1 (Be Your Own Cognitive Therapist (BYOCT) Worksheet).

- Have the client complete a small daily assignment.

- Instruct the client to read chapters 9, 10, or 11 of the workbook, when assigned.

Overview

After the first in-session exposure (chapter 7 in the workbook), treatment enters a middle phase in which sessions revolve around the routine of in-session exposures and review and assignment of *in vivo* exposures for homework. This routine is summarized in Table 8.1 in the workbook and reprinted here as Table 12.1. This is also the same routine incorporated into Worksheet 7.1. However, we recommend the BYOCT Worksheet only be used for homework exposures, as recording on the form in session disrupts the flow and takes excessive time. The session outline provided for chapter 8 of the workbook is the general outline for any in-session exposure session after the first one. As usual, each session should begin with review of the SASCI, discussion of homework from the previous week, and agenda setting.

Table 12.1 Steps for Overcoming Social Anxiety with Exposure and Cognitive Restructuring

Record responses on the BYOCT Worksheet (Worksheet 7.1) for homework exposures

Before entering the exposure situation . . .
1. Pick an anxiety-provoking situation that you would like to work on.
2. As you imagine yourself in that situation, identify the ATs and emotions caused by them.
3. Rate your belief in the ATs and identify the thinking errors within them.
4. Challenge 1–2 of the ATs with disputing questions. Be sure to answer the questions.
5. Summarize key points from answers to disputing questions into a rational response and rate your belief in the rational response.
6. Think about the situation in more detail and pick an achievable behavioral goal.

Enter the exposure situation . . .
7. Complete the exposure, using the rational response to help control your anxiety. Stay in the situation until it reaches a natural conclusion or your anxiety decreases.

After the exposure is over . . .
8. Debrief your experience in the situation:
   Did you achieve your goal?
   Did you have the ATs you expected to have?
   Did you gather any evidence about your ATs during the exposure?
   Did you gather any evidence about your rational response during the exposure?
   How well did the rational response work? Re-rate your belief in both the AT and the rational response.
9. Summarize what you can take from this experience that you can use in similar situations in the future.

Timing and Frequency of In-Session Exposures

In our research protocol, we specify that there must be at least four in-session exposures to be considered minimally sufficient, but we recommend at least six in-session exposures for the typical client. Outside of the research protocol, this middle phase can last for as long or short a time as needed, but, for individuals with clinically significant social anxiety, fewer than four exposures will rarely be adequate. The data from individuals with more generalized fears suggest that they respond to treatment at a similar rate as individuals with less generalized fears (e.g., Brown, Heimberg, & Juster, 1995; Hope, Herbert, & White,

1995). However, because they start out more impaired, they may need additional sessions to achieve high end-state functioning.

One common question is whether there should be an in-session exposure every therapy session. We recommend that at least three exposures occur right away. This allows the client to make rapid progress and reduces her anxiety about the exposures *per se*. After that, for some clients, it may be useful to devote a session to reviewing and planning *in vivo* exposures and on cognitive restructuring for particularly challenging ATs before returning to another series of consecutive exposure sessions. Depending upon the nature of the client's fears, the therapist should assign chapters 9–11 in any order that fits for the client during this time. Although not all clients will have the specific fears covered in these chapters, all are likely to benefit from the cognitive restructuring examples. The workbook material for chapters 9–11 that is most relevant to the client is usually covered in a non-exposure session. Less relevant chapters may be more briefly discussed as part of a homework review in a session in which an in-session exposure is conducted. Moreover, the amount of time devoted to discussing the material can vary widely, depending on how important it is to the presenting problem. Once the client and the therapist have observed some themes in the client's ATs, and the client has made some progress in challenging more superficial ATs, it is time to move on to advanced cognitive restructuring as described in chapter 12 of the workbook and chapter 16 of the therapist guide. The advanced cognitive restructuring work usually identifies some themes that can be the focus of the next series of exposures.

Timing and Frequency of *In Vivo* Exposures

At a minimum, clients should engage in at least one *in vivo* exposure every week. As treatment progresses, this rate should increase if possible. An initial homework assignment may involve saying hello and one other thing to a coworker. This can evolve into several more extended conversations per week as the client makes progress. In fact, following the second exposure, the workbook (p. 160) recommends a small daily assignment to establish a pattern of regularly facing feared situations.

This same assignment is continued through the rest of treatment and usually becomes such a habit that the client no longer considers it homework.

Other Homework Assignments

Homework may also involve activities that will facilitate future assignments. Highly socially anxious and avoidant clients may have limited their opportunities to engage with other people. Thus, a homework assignment might include inquiries about activities involving other people such as a class or a community or religious activity. Clients without jobs due to social anxiety may have homework assignments to seek job opportunities. If these activities are themselves anxiety-provoking, they may serve as *in vivo* exposures. More often they are additional assignments while the *in vivo* exposures serve as preparation for taking advantage of the new activities.

Reviewing Homework for *In Vivo* Exposures

For clients to benefit from this treatment, they must begin to engage in anxiety-provoking activities in their daily lives. It is essential that therapists encourage this by carefully assigning and reviewing homework for *in vivo* exposure. At the beginning of each session, the therapist should review the client's completed Worksheet 7.1 and comment on aspects that show progress or use of cognitive restructuring skills. The client should be given a brief opportunity to relate her experience in exposure, celebrating successes, and resolving challenges with the therapist's assistance. In sessions with a planned in-session exposure, this discussion will necessarily be somewhat limited. In non-exposure sessions, it may form the basis for much of the session as the therapist guides the client in further cognitive restructuring activities based on the homework exposure experience.

If the client is not completing *in vivo* exposure assignments, this is a serious problem that should be addressed with increasing urgency.

The first step may be to remind the client of the rationale for *in vivo* exposure (pp. 125–126 of the workbook). Check that she appreciates that facing fears in real life is an essential component of overcoming social anxiety. The second step may be to clarify why the client is apparently agreeing to do the homework in session but then not following through. Perhaps the assignments seem too difficult or not relevant to the client's long-term treatment goals. Perhaps the client is overly focused upon the risks of making changes and needs to review some of the important reasons for change from chapter 1 of the workbook to enhance motivation. The final step would be to insist on greater compliance with homework exposures before proceeding further in therapy. This step is needed only infrequently and typically involves devoting extra session time to preparing for the *in vivo* exposure, through repetition of in-session exposures and/or cognitive restructuring.

Occasionally, clients will do the *in vivo* exposure but not the cognitive restructuring on the BYOCT Worksheet. The therapist should encourage the cognitive restructuring in preparation for the exposure as some of the debriefing can be done in the therapy session. If homework exposure seems to be going well and the client is excited about her progress, then the therapist should use his or her judgment regarding the utility of the BYOCT Worksheet for this particular client.

Reviewing SASCI Scores

The SASCI should be administered each week and reviewed to monitor overall progress. It is not unusual to see an increase in scores in the middle of treatment as clients began to reduce their avoidance. They may believe their anxiety is getting worse because they are experiencing more of it on a daily basis. This trend should reverse as treatment continues. If the SASCI scores do not seem to match progress that is apparent from the review of homework and client's report in session, then the therapist should review the instructions on the SASCI to make sure ratings are in comparison to when the client began treatment.

Qualitative Changes in Treatment Procedures Over the Course of Multiple Exposures

Although the activities are largely the same through the middle portion of treatment that involves repeated in-session and *in vivo* exposures combined with cognitive restructuring, there are qualitative changes in the procedures. These changes culminate in the advanced cognitive restructuring activities of chapter 12 in the client workbook and end with the beginning of the termination phase. These qualitative changes occur along the following dimensions:

- Less anxiety-provoking to more anxiety-provoking situations

- More reliance on the therapist to more reliance on the client for cognitive restructuring

- More in-session exposures to more *in vivo* exposures

- Less complex situations to more complex situations

- More reliance on the therapist to more reliance on the client to pick exposure situations

- Cognitive restructuring focused on more superficial ATs and anxiety to greater focus on core beliefs and other emotions (e.g., shame)

Thus, the overall flow of treatment is to move from therapist guidance to greater client guidance. The ultimate goal is for the client to have all of the necessary tools to continue to manage anxiety-provoking situations as they arise after therapy ends. We expect clients to continue to make progress on their own. However, as they enter new situations made possible by their progress, they may need to cope with increased anxiety. For example, one client returned to see one of us about 6 months after treatment had ended because he was very anxious about asking his girlfriend to marry him. This was an entirely new situation for a man in his 30s who had never dated prior to entering treatment. Reminding him to apply the same skills to this new situation helped reduce his anxiety to manageable levels.

Another advantage of empowering clients is that they have the tools to face other challenges in their lives. For example, the cognitive restructuring activities are helpful for all types of stress and depression. Learning to break challenges into smaller pieces and gradually overcome them, as is done with exposure, may help the client to master a new career or deal with difficult life events.

In practical terms, these qualitative changes mean that, in later sessions, the therapist asks the client what situation would be helpful to focus on for in-session exposure, perhaps from an array of possibilities. For example, a therapist might say something like the following:

> We have been working on your dating fears. I am wondering if you feel like you need one more exposure in preparation for the date you have scheduled this weekend or if we should move in a different direction. You have also told me that anxiety about interviews is keeping you from moving to a better job. We could work on that as well.

For greater client control of cognitive restructuring, the therapist might say:

> As we have worked on making presentations, one AT that keeps coming up has to do with appearing competent. Why don't you start to walk through the cognitive restructuring steps for addressing that AT? I'll jump in and assist as needed.

The therapist then allows the client to work through the cognitive restructuring, assisting if the client gets stuck or offering evidence in support of a point (e.g., "Another piece of evidence that you are competent is that good employee evaluation you received a couple of weeks ago").

The nature of the AT selected for cognitive restructuring changes over the course of treatment as well. Initially, more superficial ATs are selected; later, ATs are more related to core beliefs. This is a complex issue that will be discussed in more detail below.

How to Know Which AT to Focus On for Cognitive Restructuring

Perhaps the most difficult aspect of cognitive-behavioral therapy for inexperienced therapists is judging which AT will result in the most productive cognitive restructuring. Prior to the exposure, the client lists a number of ATs. Given time constraints, only one (or occasionally two) AT is followed through all the steps of cognitive restructuring. Our experience training new therapists has revealed that, as experienced clinicians with cognitive-behavioral therapy (CBT) for social anxiety, we often have a consensus on which AT to pick. It is difficult to articulate the implicit rules about why one AT seems more useful to target than another at a given point in treatment. We have tried to address this question empirically.

In chapter 9, we described a study of the themes present in ATs of individuals with social anxiety disorder who received our group treatment (Hope, Burns et al., 2010). The second part of the study involved identifying the types of ATs selected by the therapist for cognitive restructuring across the first four exposures for each client and the relation of this decision to clinical outcome. Therapists tended to follow our recommendation and selected objective, situationally based performance ATs for the first exposure. ATs such as "I won't know what to say" can be easily disputed by actual performance in the role-played exposure. This strategy was associated with a positive clinical outcome in our data. ATs related to negative self-evaluation (negative self-labels like "incompetent" or "boring") or concerns about performance such as not knowing what to say were most likely to be selected for cognitive restructuring later in treatment, except for the fourth exposure, when therapists appeared to shift to other-referent ATs that focused on other people reactions to the client ("She'll think I'm boring."). This pattern could indicate a shift in strategy from challenging whether a particular AT such as "I'm boring" is accurate to focusing on the consequences of an AT—"So what if she thinks you are boring?" Interestingly, it appeared that focusing too early on these evaluations by others (as opposed to self-evaluations) was associated with poorer clinical outcome.

ATs about experiencing anxiety were rarely selected by therapists in our study. This is consistent with the notion that the experience of anxiety will take care of itself with repeated exposure. The greatest concern should be any perceived negative consequences. When therapists did focus on ATs related to experiencing anxiety, this was associated with a poor clinical outcome. It is impossible to determine from these correlational data whether clients who are overly concerned about experiencing anxiety do less well in the therapy or whether focusing on those ATs, at the expense of other themes, is problematic. In the absence of further data, we recommend against spending extended restructuring efforts on ATs such as "My heart will pound" or "I'll blush." It will be more productive to focus on ATs about the consequences of those symptoms such as the meaning of a pounding heart or how others might respond if the symptom is visible.

Although chapter 12 of the workbook (chapter 16 in the therapist guide) is focused on identifying core beliefs, many clients move more quickly toward work on core beliefs, especially if the therapist is able to focus the cognitive restructuring efficiently and attempts to elicit ATs that underlie the initial ones that might be reported. There should be a clear progression from more superficial ATs (e.g., "I won't know what to say") to the underlying fears (e.g., "I know I can always talk about the weather but I won't be seen as intelligent if I can't talk about important topics") to core beliefs (e.g., "I'm not smart and people won't like me when they figure that out"). It is perfectly acceptable to identify and challenge core beliefs earlier, if the client is able to do so. This might also involve assigning the reading of chapter 12 of the workbook ahead of schedule. The pace of the cognitive work should depend on the client's ability to make cognitive changes, not forced by trying to focus on central, difficult-to-change core beliefs before the client has had success at changing more superficial ATs. See Persons (2008) for more discussion on identifying and changing core beliefs.

How to Pace the Difficulty of In-Session and *In Vivo* Exposures

When considering how quickly to move from easier to more difficult situations in either in-session or homework exposures, keep in mind that the typical client with moderately severe social anxiety disorder has a positive clinical outcome with approximately four to five in-session exposures and weekly *in vivo* exposures across approximately eight to 10 sessions. This means the difficulty of exposures increases fairly rapidly over time. In chapters 9–11 of the workbook, we outline a typical course of exposures for the type of situation covered in each chapter. Since most clients will have fears in multiple domains, the focus of the exposure will change across time.

Outside of a research protocol, the pace can be more leisurely. However, our clinical experience suggests that clients do better if they see early progress. Nothing is more convincing that the stress of exposure is worthwhile than success in situations that were previously seen as unattainable. Less severe clients are likely to become bored or impatient if progress is too slow. On the other hand, clients are likely to avoid situations they perceive as too challenging.

External Role Players

In individual treatment, the therapist serves as the role player or audience member for many, if not all, in-session exposures. One of the advantages of group treatment is that other group members are available to take on these roles. Depending on the setting, other individuals may be available to assist. Most often these external role players will be other staff in the clinical setting. Fellow clinicians are often willing to step in for a 10-min role play if the scheduling is arranged in advance. The client's session time can be scheduled to facilitate access to external role players. We have occasionally had clerical staff serve as audience members for public speaking exposures. In teaching settings, trainees often enjoy participating in the session. Obviously, any external role players need to be known to the clinician and fully briefed on the maintenance of confidentiality.

When external role players will be coming into the session, we give the client a general idea of who they are and assurance that confidentiality extends to that person. Immediately prior to the exposure, the therapist steps out of the room and briefs the role player on the situation, giving instructions about how friendly he or she should act, and so forth. It is also helpful to inform external role players about the interruptions for Subjective Units of Discomfort Scale (SUDS) ratings and ask them to prompt the interaction if the SUDS probe disrupts the flow of the interaction (e.g., "You were saying something about the movie you saw . . ."). If the role player has time, the therapist may ask him or her to remain briefly after the exposure, as clients often want feedback on their performance. The external role player may participate in the performance and anxiety ratings described below. Although role players should always be instructed to be honest in any feedback, they should also be instructed to avoid highly critical feedback.

Cognitive Restructuring Techniques

Over the years we have developed and adopted a variety of strategies to make particular points in cognitive restructuring. Examples are scattered throughout the case examples in the client workbook. Rather than repeat all of the information here, we will review the strategies and indicate where an extended example can be located.

Pie Chart to Analyze the Likelihood of Multiple Reactions or Outcomes

One common theme in ATs is excessive focus on one possible negative outcome or reaction when a variety of possibilities are viable. An example would be ATs related to the concern that others will notice anxiety symptoms and draw a negative conclusion, such as the person being mentally ill. Another example would be reasons someone might refuse a request, such as an invitation for a date. Often the goal of cognitive restructuring is to help the client see that there are many possible outcomes, reactions, or reasons, not just the catastrophic one originally identified by the client. The therapist can make this point by asking the client to estimate the likelihood (out of 100) that various options are true and then putting these percentages into a pie chart. This exercise often leads to a rational response that there is only an X% chance of the AT being true. See pages 178–183 of the workbook for an extended example of this technique. It is also discussed further in chapter 14 of this therapist guide.

Continuum of Negative Events to Gain Perspective on the Seriousness of a Reaction or Outcome

Often ATs are related to catastrophic interpretations of ordinary events or outcomes. Often the client overestimates the risk and underestimates the potential pay-off for a given situation. A powerful technique to provide perspective on the real risk is to consider the possible negative outcome in the context of other negative life events. This is done by developing a continuum. First the therapist draws a line on the board. On the extreme left end, the therapist puts a mildly negative event such as stubbing one's toe. On the extreme right, the therapist asks the client to identify the most catastrophic event possible, typically something like losing one's entire family in an automobile accident. The client is then asked to place one or more feared outcomes related to her social anxiety on the continuum. This exercise often leads to a rational response related to being able to live with the feared consequences. See pages 186–187 of the workbook for an extended example of this technique.

Lists of Evidence For and Against a Conclusion

One of the disputing questions asks for evidence for and against a particular AT. This can be further developed by building two parallel lists on the board. The therapist starts with the column that reflects the AT (e.g., "Evidence you are incompetent"). Then the therapist and the client work to fill in the other column (e.g., "Evidence you are competent"). This strategy often results in a rational response that summarizes the evidence for the second column (e.g., "There is plenty of good evidence I am competent").

To make the comparison most effective, the therapist must choose the column titles in such a way to ensure that the second list is longer than the first one. The relative physical length of the columns is surprisingly compelling. The therapist can contribute items to both lists but typically only does so for the second one. Any therapist contribution should not be added to the board unless the client agrees, even grudgingly, that it is appropriate.

Comparative Ratings of Anxiety and Performance

There are several studies that suggest that socially anxious individuals underestimate the quality of their performance and overestimate the visibility of their anxiety in feared situations (e.g., Norton & Hope,

2001). That discrepancy decreases with successful treatment (Hope, Heimberg, & Bruch, 1995) as socially anxious individuals' ratings move closer to those of observers. Therapists can take advantage of clients' biases by having the client, the therapist, and any other observers/role players make ratings of various aspects of performance or anxiety in a role play. Typically ratings are made on a 0–100 scale, analogous to the SUDS scale. The most common ratings are "how well you did" and "how anxious you looked."

There are three keys to making this intervention a success. First, the therapist should write the scale on the board. Anxious clients (and occasionally role players) may misunderstand a scale that is explained verbally. Second, endpoint scale anchors must be carefully chosen to avoid perfectionist goals and generate the desired discrepancy between observers and the client. Third, the therapist must be extremely clear that everyone will record his or her ratings silently on a sheet of paper. There is a tendency to blurt out ratings. In individual treatment, the sheets are given to the client, who reads the ratings aloud. In group treatment, group members can reveal their ratings one at a time.

Here are some common examples of these types of ratings:

"How well did you do in the conversation?"

0 = Dismal failure; no one is likely to want to talk with you

100 = Typical conversation that the average person might have

"How anxious did you appear during the speech?"

0 = The amount of energy and stress the average person would experience in this situation

100 = Extremely anxious; looked as if you could definitely not continue and might even need medical attention

Videotape Feedback (with Cognitive Preparation)

Another potentially powerful intervention is videotape feedback (Harvey, Clark, Ehlers, & Rapee, 2000). The in-session exposure is videotaped. Clients are asked to predict, in detail, what they believe they will see in the video (using numerical ratings of specific behaviors), to clearly visualize how they came across, and to watch the video as if they were watching a stranger (to gain some distance from the emotional memory of the exposure). After viewing the videotape with the therapist, the client is asked to give new numerical ratings describing her performance and/or the level of her anxiety. Client ratings typically indicate a higher quality performance and lower level of anxiety than the client had imagined prior to viewing the videotape. However, this procedure appears to be most effective for clients whose perception of their performance is most discrepant from that of observers (Rodebaugh, 2004; Rodebaugh & Chambless, 2002).

Solutions to Common Difficulties

Client Does Not Become Anxious During In-Session Exposures

Occasionally clients will experience little anxiety during in-session exposures and/or suggest that they are not sufficiently realistic. This is less of a problem than most therapists expect. After all, having a conversation with someone poses similar behavioral demands regardless of whether the conversation partner is real or role playing. In that sense, many in-session exposures differ from real life only in the sense that the therapist can control the process and outcome. On the other hand, some situations are more difficult to stage effectively than are others. Fears of presentations to large groups of people may not be evoked if the audience consists of only one to two people.

Clients often use a subtle type of avoidance to control their anxiety in role-played exposures. By telling themselves the situation is not real or does not "count," they can avoid experiencing anxiety (and prevent themselves from deriving much benefit). On page 133 of the workbook, we described this strategy as analogous to trying to learn to swim but never letting go of the side of the pool. Fortunately, this situation offers an excellent example of the power of the cognitive model. It is not the situation, but how one interprets it, that causes anxiety. The therapist should explicitly label the strategy as avoidance. The therapist then encourages the client to throw herself more fully into the situation by acting as if it were real. It is often worthwhile to query clients about minor changes in the role play that might help it be more realistic to them as well.

If the client fails to become anxious during in-session exposures because the situation is not genuinely realistic, then the therapist should attempt to make it more so. Specific strategies for this are discussed in the context of various situations for chapters 9–11 of the workbook. If this continues to be a problem and the therapist runs out of ideas, then it might be useful to consult colleagues. One often sees even very experienced clinicians using professional listservs to get broader help at brainstorming ways to make exposure more effective. Obviously, this is done with care to maintain a client's confidentiality.

Client Becomes Increasingly Fearful of In-Session Exposures

Typically, clients become increasingly comfortable with the exposure procedures as treatment progresses. The specific situations may (and should) evoke substantial anxiety. However, usually they have clearly invested in facing their fears, and, to some extent, they actively seek exposures. If the opposite is occurring, then the therapist should discuss it explicitly with the client, listening carefully to the client's subjective experience in anticipation of, during, and after exposures. Exposures may be proceeding too quickly, and the client may be feeling overwhelmed. Additional anxiety management strategies may be needed such as relaxation, breathing retraining, or medication. Insufficient attention may have been given to the postexposure debriefing, resulting in the client's perception that the role plays were failures rather than successes.

Client Seems to Be Making No Progress with Cognitive Restructuring

Occasionally clients will cling fervently to ATs despite repeatedly being able to acknowledge evidence against their validity. For example, a client might say, "I know my hand shaking is not as visible as I think it is, but I still worry about it." A client with fears of public speaking might say, "I know I have never had to run out of the room during a speech, but I cannot help worrying about what would happen if I did." If this continues across several sessions of cognitive restructuring and is clearly preventing further progress, then it is often useful to ask the client two questions: How is maintaining this belief useful for her? and What would it take to give up the belief? A nonconfrontational approach, such as is used in motivational interviewing (e.g., Miller & Rollnick, 2002), and reliance on the strength of the therapeutic alliance to avoid triggering fears of negative evaluation can be very effective.

Client Is Unable to Report ATs

In earlier chapters, we discussed strategies for assisting clients who have difficulty identifying ATs. A few clients, however, are unable to identify any ATs, even in the context of anxiety-provoking exposures in the session. If this problem persists through one or two exposures, then it is time to de-emphasize the cognitive aspects of the treatment and focus on exposure. Exposure without cognitive restructuring is a viable intervention (e.g., Feske & Chambless, 1995). Goal setting and debriefing the exposure should be continued. Rather than explicitly discussing ATs, the debriefing can focus on the client's subjective experience and process any objective information on the quality of performance or visibility of symptoms. Some of the time previously devoted to cognitive restructuring prior to the exposure can be devoted to graphing the anticipated SUDS pattern. Comparing expected anxiety with actual anxiety can also be a helpful debriefing exercise.

Clients may feel they are failing the treatment program if they are unable to identify ATs for cognitive restructuring. The therapist can help alleviate these concerns by explaining that cognitive restructuring is only one of several tools to help manage anxiety but it does not work for everyone. Exposure is likely to be helpful on its own. Indeed, the bulk of the research evidence suggests that exposure is the most powerful change agent in this intervention (Emge & Hope, 2010).

Client Is Using Subtle Avoidance or Safety Behaviors During Exposures

Often therapists will note that clients are using safety behaviors during exposures. For example, a client might avoid eye contact, wear certain clothes so perspiration does not show, stick to certain "safe" conversation topics, over-rely on notes for public speaking, or avoid self-disclosure. In this case, the therapist can discuss it during the post-exposure processing and then be sure to incorporate dropping these safety behaviors during the homework for *in vivo* exposure or in the next in-session exposure. Sometimes this might create an artificial exposure in session as it might be helpful to exaggerate the lack of safety behaviors. Someone who avoids eye contact could be asked to make continuous excessive eye contact or someone who avoids self-disclosure could monopolize the conversation about themselves. Typically the cognitive restructuring work revolves around feared outcomes if the safety behaviors are not used.

Chapter 13 | *Exposure and Cognitive Restructuring: Conversation Fears*

(Corresponds to chapter 9 of the workbook)

Timeline

Variable

Materials Needed

- Copy of client workbook

- Dry erase board

- Social Anxiety Session Change Index (SASCI)

- Weekly Social Anxiety Session Change Graph (same copy as used last session)

- Table 5.1 (List of Thinking Errors)

- Figure 6.1 (Disputing Questions)

- Form for Recording Key Information During In-Session Exposures That Can Serve as Session Progress Note

- Worksheet 7.1 (Be Your Own Cognitive Therapist (BYOCT) Worksheet)

Session Outline

- Administer, score, and graph the SASCI

- Review homework

- Briefly review psychoeducation on small talk

- Do in-session cognitive restructuring and exposure

- Assign homework

Homework

- Have the client complete exposure homework including Worksheet 7.1 (Be Your Own Cognitive Therapist (BYOCT) Worksheet).

- Instruct the client to continue small daily assignments.

- Instruct the client to read chapter 10 of the workbook.

Overview of Chapters 9, 10, and 11 in the Client Workbook

Chapters 9, 10, and 11 of the client workbook focus on specific types of feared situations—fears of conversations in chapter 9, observational fears in chapter 10, and fears of public speaking in chapter 11. It is recommended that all three of these chapters be assigned to all clients at some point after chapter 8 has been covered. Irrespective of the specific social anxieties that the client brings to treatment, some of the automatic thoughts and treatment techniques covered in each chapter are likely to be relevant. These three chapters are presented in an order that recognizes that clients most commonly present for treatment of generalized social anxiety that includes fear of conversations with others. However, the order that these three chapters are assigned may be varied so that clients first read the one most relevant to their presenting complaint (e.g., chapter 11 would be read first by the client presenting primarily with fear relating to public speaking).

Psychoeducation

Most individuals who seek treatment for social anxiety have at least some difficulty with casual conversations or "small talk." Chapter 9 in the workbook opens with psychoeducational material about the importance of small talk in everyday life.

Designing In-Session Exposures

Conversational situations are often the easiest exposures to design. They typically require few props, and a variety of circumstances can be easily staged. Changes in the topic, purpose of the conversation, and role player behavior create an infinite number of possible exposures. However, many of the behaviors in casual conversations and dating are strongly influenced by culture. The therapist should always consider the client's culture and values when designing in-session exposures. For example, female clients may adhere to cultural norms about the appropriateness of asking a man for a date that need to be distinguished from avoidance behavior. We will discuss a few common role-play scenarios that may require extra planning or strategies.

Avoiding Escape Behavior

Socially anxious individuals with fears of casual conversations have often become highly skilled at terminating conversations quickly. In the initial role plays, the therapist may have to emphasize the importance of continuing the conversation despite anxiety and prompt the client to continue if he attempts to escape. In initial exposures, the role player may need to provide assistance by introducing conversation topics to keep the exposure going.

Many conversations have a specific purpose that can lead the role play to a natural conclusion. For example, a conversation in which the client is to invite someone to have coffee can rapidly draw to a conclusion once the invitation is made. Anxious clients may blurt out the request immediately to escape the exposure. If such behavior is likely, the therapist should instruct the client that he cannot make the request until after the therapist gives the signal to do so. This requires the client to build up to the request naturally and increases the chances that the actual request will be made with greater social skill. If possible given the circumstances, the client should be informed that the role play will continue after the request as well. For example, if someone refuses an invitation, the client needs to continue the conversation, not just abruptly depart. If the person accepts the invitation, then further conversation can focus on working out the logistical details.

Silences

A common fear in conversations is that there will be an extended silence and the client will be unable to break it. Socially anxious individuals' perception of their ability to break the silence, of the degree of their individual responsibility for breaking the silence, and of the duration of conversational silences is often greatly distorted. The Achievable Behavioral Goal can be to break the silence. The role player is then instructed to allow a silence to develop and not to break it no matter how long it lasts. This exposure is often accompanied by an estimate by the client prior to the role play of the likely duration of a long silence. These estimates are typically exaggerated but should not be challenged ahead of time. The therapist times any silences, asks for another estimate of the duration of the silence after the role play, and then provides the client with the actual data. Both the client's success at breaking the silence and the concrete evidence of the overestimation of its duration can yield good rational responses (e.g., "Silences feel much longer than they are"; "I can probably come up with something to restart the conversation"). In debriefing the exposure, it is useful to discuss the social pressure to break silences, and the role player may describe how uncomfortable it is to sit in silence. This can be further evidence that most conversation partners will work hard to break silences and that breaking the silence is not entirely the client's responsibility.

Starting or Joining Conversations

Some aspects of conversations are similar to the specific social phobias in that they are very short. If a client fears starting or joining a conversation but has little anxiety once it is started, then effective exposure will focus on only the aspects that are feared. For example, the client may be asked to go from one person to the next as if moving from conversation to conversation at a party. If only the therapist is available as a role player, then he or she needs to enact the role of a different person each time the client starts the conversation. Typically the client is instructed to initiate the conversation, and the therapist terminates the interaction as soon as it is started. An example of this type of exposure is described as part of the case of Penny in chapter 9 of the workbook.

Typical Automatic Thoughts and Cognitive Restructuring

Chapter 9 in the workbook covers three typical automatic thoughts (ATs) for conversations: not knowing what to say, not having anything interesting to say, and having poor conversational skills. Socially anxious individuals are often quite adamant that they have a deficit in social skills. As noted previously, however, research shows they underestimate the quality of their performance (Norton & Hope, 2001). Although social skill deficits are occasionally present and socially anxious individuals may perform slightly more poorly than nonanxious individuals (Norton & Hope, 2001), in our experience, most have reasonably adequate skills but anxiety interferes with their ability to execute them. Some apparent social skill deficits, such as poor eye contact, may be conceptualized as avoidance of the anxiety caused by making eye contact. As the anxiety decreases, the client's behavior improves. Occasionally clients will need to be encouraged to fully face their fears by avoiding avoidance behaviors. In this example, making eye contact can become an achievable behavioral goal during exposures.

Nothing changes a socially anxious individual's belief that he cannot make casual conversation so much as repeated success at doing so. The role of cognitive restructuring is to prepare the client to enter the situation to test the validity of the specific ATs about conversational skills. Post-exposure cognitive restructuring often centers on overcoming the tendency to disqualify successes and preparing to apply the lessons learned to future conversations.

Once ATs about the quality of the client's performance in conversation are addressed, it often becomes clear that the underlying ATs relate to expectations of rejection. Repeated conversations imply that people will get to know one another better. Socially anxious individuals may fear that intimacy will lead to closer relationships for which they feel unprepared or that will ultimately lead to rejection. Such ATs are closer to the core beliefs that are addressed in chapter 12 of the workbook. Moving from superficial ATs about performance to these core beliefs is a sign of progress in therapy.

Homework for *In Vivo* Exposure

Homework for *in vivo* exposure to conversational fears parallels the in-session exposures. In fact, in-session exposures are often rehearsals for a desired *in vivo* opportunity. Several complications that may arise are described in the sections that follow.

Extreme Social Isolation

Clients who have been highly avoidant of social interaction may engage in very few social contacts a day. In such cases, it is important to increase the frequency of contact as quickly as possible. We usually initiate the daily homework assignment of "saying hello and one other thing to someone not normally spoken with" every day. This can be increased to several times a day, as it takes little time. No matter how socially isolated a client may be, he can make a trip to a store or other public place and greet whoever is there. Additional homework assignments involve asking clients to look into various organizations or groups that they will join in order to facilitate their treatment. Over the years, our socially anxious clients have chosen to increase their contact with others by joining health clubs, religious groups, activity-oriented clubs (e.g., book, hiking, biking, sailing), singles groups, volunteer organizations, adult education classes, and so forth. In-session exposures may address barriers to joining such organizations by role playing an interaction at the first meeting or even the first phone call that the client needs to make to get more information about the group.

Dating

Individuals with social anxiety disorder marry later, if at all (Schneier, Johnson, Hornig, Liebowitz, & Weissman, 1992), and many seek treatment with the hope of increasing comfort with potential dating partners and developing an intimate relationship. Certainly, the various stages of dating from initial conversations to requests for dates to expressing positive feelings can be role played in session. It is often appropriate to address dating assertiveness skills, such as refusing advances, as well. Treatment becomes more difficult if the client does not have potential dating partners in his social circle, as is often the case. If this seems likely to be a problem, then fairly early in treatment, homework assignments (and in-session exposures) should center on getting involved in organizations or activities that will bring contact with potential dating partners. Great caution should be exercised when using dating services or Internet personal ads to achieve this goal. Better options are organizations like the ones suggested above for decreasing social isolation, such as community or religious organizations or singles groups that have an additional focus (e.g., ski club).

Most dating issues are similar for heterosexual and gay, lesbian, or bisexual socially anxious individuals. We have successfully worked with gay, lesbian, and bisexual clients in both individual and group treatment. The therapist should be familiar with the dating opportunities and norms for a particular community. A realistic assessment needs to be made of the person's physical and social risk of being more open about his sexual orientation.

Typical Course of In-Session and *In Vivo* Exposures

The course of treatment should always be highly individualized and proceed on a course and pace appropriate for a given socially anxious client. However, it is possible to outline a sequence of exposures that is fairly typical for someone seeking treatment for fears of conversations and dating:

Exposure #1: Conversation with the therapist acting in the role of a stranger in a neutral setting, such as standing in line at a store.

Homework: Greeting and saying one other thing to two to three people during the week with whom the client would not normally talk.

Exposure #2: Longer conversation with the therapist as a stranger in a neutral setting; the therapist may take less responsibility for keeping the conversation going without being unfriendly. Homework: Conversation that is more than just a greeting with someone who is not a potential dating partner. Daily greetings and saying one other thing to people with whom the client would not normally talk. Begin to make inquiries about community college classes (or other similar venues) for later exposures.

Exposure #3: Conversation with the therapist (or external role player) who is a potential dating partner or friend at the first day of community college class. Homework: Conversation with someone who could be a potential dating partner. Continue daily greetings and follow up on creating opportunities for socialization.

Exposure #4: Conversation with the therapist (or external role player) who is a potential dating partner; conversation includes a feared outcome, such as an extended silence. Homework: Two or three conversations with someone who could be a potential dating partner. Increase frequency of daily greetings and follow up on opportunities for socialization.

Exposure #5: Requesting a casual date (movie, lunch) with either the therapist or the external role player. The first time the person accepts the date (do not inform the client of the outcome ahead of time). At subsequent session, repeat the exposure with the person declining the date. Homework: Invite someone, not necessarily a potential dating partner, for a very casual event, such as getting together for coffee or having lunch. Continue daily greetings and follow up on opportunities for socialization.

Exposure #6: Being on a date with someone, often having dinner or dessert after seeing a movie together. Homework: Requesting and going on a date with someone.

Exposure #7: Expressing positive feelings to someone (e.g., "I have really enjoyed being with you and would like to see you again").

Homework: Requesting a date with someone, expressing positive feelings if appropriate.

As noted earlier, not every session includes an in-session exposure, so these seven suggested exposures could happen over 10 or more sessions. Sessions without in-session exposures would focus on cognitive restructuring and problem solving getting involved in opportunities for socialization. Homework for nonexposure sessions would be *in vivo* exposures of increasing difficulty and logically fall between the in-session exposures.

Chapter 14 — *Exposure and Cognitive Restructuring: Observational Fears*

(Corresponds to chapter 10 of the workbook)

Timeline

Variable

Materials Needed

- Copy of client workbook
- Dry erase board
- Social Anxiety Session Change Index (SASCI)
- Weekly Social Anxiety Session Change Graph (same copy as used last session)
- Worksheet 14.1 (Pie Chart Technique)
- Table 5.1 (List of Thinking Errors)
- Figure 6.1 (Disputing Questions)
- Form for Recording Key Information During In-Session Exposures That Can Serve as Session Progress Note
- Worksheet 7.1 (Be Your Own Cognitive Therapist (BYOCT) Worksheet)

Session Outline

- Administer, score, and graph the SASCI
- Review homework

- Briefly review psychoeducation on specific social phobias

- Do in-session cognitive restructuring and exposure

- Assign homework

Homework

- Have the client complete exposure homework including Worksheet 7.1 (Be Your Own Cognitive Therapist (BYOCT) Worksheet).

- Instruct the client to continue small daily assignments.

- Instruct the client to read chapter 11 of the workbook.

Psychoeducation

Chapter 10 opens with an assessment of observational fears and some psychoeducational material about the specific social phobias. Although many socially anxious individuals have some of these fears, they are less common as primary complaints in treatment-seeking samples than are more generalized fears of conversations and public speaking. Research suggests that the specific social phobias are quite responsive to cognitive-behavioral therapy (CBT; e.g., Mattick, Peters, & Clarke, 1989). This chapter can also be very useful when treating performance fears such as those experienced by musicians or athletes.

Individuals with specific social phobias may be quite ashamed of the problem because simple, everyday behaviors have become difficult. The material on self-consciousness and the disruption of the automaticity of overlearned behaviors can help reduce this shame by providing an explanation for uneven performance.

Pie Chart Technique

Chapter 10 introduces the pie chart as a tool for helping clients to examine catastrophic fears. In chapter 10, the pie chart was used to help

Miguel work on the ATs "My hand will shake," "The customer will see my hand shake," and "The customer will think I am incompetent and not give us any business." As in this example, the therapist begins by encouraging the client to consider a variety of neutral (e.g., my hand will shake but the client will not notice) and less negative alternatives (e.g., he will think that I have the flu) to the feared catastrophe (e.g., he will think I am incompetent) and asks the client to assign percentages of the pie chart to those alternatives first. In this way, the therapist has strategically left a relatively small percentage of likelihood for the remaining negative outcomes.

As noted in the workbook, the pie chart can also be used for ATs associated with catastrophic fears relating to speaking in public (e.g., the audience will believe I am incompetent if I cannot answer all of their questions) and social interaction (e.g., she will think I am a loser and reject me if I blush) as well. Moreover, therapists may find the pie chart useful any time a client has ATs that contain catastrophic thinking errors that predict something terribly bad is going to happen when, in reality, there are many possible outcomes. Worksheet 14.1 is a form that may be used in session or given to a client as a homework assignment for challenging an AT containing a catastrophic thinking error.

Worksheet 14.1 Pie Chart Technique

Briefly describe the situation:

List Catastrophic AT:

List as many alternative explanations as possible. Come up with at least 7-10 other possibilities. (Ask: What other alternatives are possible other than the feared catastrophe?):

Rate the percentage likelihood that the first alternative could be true and fill in the corresponding area below. Repeat for the next alternative explanation. Lastly, rate the percentage likelihood of the most feared outcome. Each piece of the pie represents 10%. Any alternative can be rated as more or less than 10% by shading the desired area.

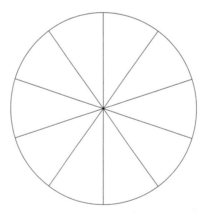

Rational Response based on the Pie Chart:

Brief Situations

Most of the specific social phobias are very brief situations that do not initially seem amenable to exposure. Signing one's name or taking a drink of coffee require only a few seconds, not long enough for habituation to occur. The solution is to set up circumstances for repeated occurrences of the behavior. For example, someone with fears of signing her name can do so dozens of times during a 5-min in-session exposure. The repeated nature of the exposure may not be a true representation of the way things happen in the real world, but each individual signature certainly can be. There are several strategies for setting up the repeated occurrences for in-session exposures:

- In group treatment or if one or more extra role players are available, the client can move from one person to the next repeating the feared behavior. For example, each person could hold a clipboard and request that the client sign her name each time. Each person could hold a glass of water from which the client drinks or a glass into which the client pours water.

- For eating and drinking fears, a restaurant situation can be simulated with real food and drink. The client continues to take bites or sips throughout the ongoing conversation. The difficulty can be adjusted by manipulating the nature of the food and/or drink (salads, spaghetti, hot drinks) or the utensils (chopsticks or tall awkward wine glasses).

- The client can perform the behavior repeatedly in front of the therapist. The therapist can become more or less threatening depending on how close to the client he or she stands, how much attention he or she pays to the client's performance, and whether he or she makes any comments about the client's anxiety.

Incorporating Feared Outcomes

Very often individuals with specific social phobias need to have their feared outcome occur in an in-session exposure. For example, the person with fears of spilling food or drink needs to actually spill something. In many cases, exaggerating the symptom can be a powerful intervention for clients who fear losing control. They quickly realize one of two points: that the feared outcome is much less likely than they imagined or that the feared outcome is not a catastrophe. Here are some examples of how to incorporate feared outcomes into in-session exposures for specific social phobias:

- For fears of spilling, the client can purposefully pour a glass to overflowing while someone is holding it or purposefully spill water on themselves or someone else. A towel can be placed on the carpet or the role play partner if needed.

- For fears of making mistakes, the client can purposefully make mistakes. For example, the client can purposefully type the wrong keys, write incorrectly or unevenly on the board or easel, or start coughing excessively after taking a drink of water.

- For fears of shaking, the client can purposefully exaggerate the shaking while engaged in the feared situation.

Clients are often quite hesitant to face the feared outcomes, and this is not appropriate for a first exposure. The client must have a great deal of trust in the therapist to not be humiliated by the experience. The greater is the exaggeration, the more effective is the exposure. The therapist may have to strongly encourage the client to achieve success. For example, it is much better to spill a cup of water than a single drop. More often than not, the exposure ends with laughter as the client gives in to the outlandishness of the situation.

Fears of Using Public Restrooms

It is essential to distinguish between difficulty using public restrooms because of fears of contamination, as would be found in obsessive-compulsive disorder, and performance anxiety, as in a specific social phobia. Known as paruresis, and often referred to as "bashful bladder," anxiety and avoidance about urinating in the presence of others typically occurs in men and usually involves fears of using urinals. Quite often this is the only fear present when men seek treatment. As noted in the workbook, it can be quite disabling if avoidance has become extensive. This presentation of social anxiety disorder is fairly uncommon, but our experience suggests it responds to similar CBT interventions (see Soifer, Zgourides, Himle, & Pickering, 2001, for a manual specifically devoted to the cognitive-behavioral treatment of paruresis). There are a few considerations when treating this fear, however.

The first consideration is the gender of the therapist. The treatment is greatly complicated if the therapist cannot enter the lavatory with the client. Although the therapist will maintain a discrete distance to allow the client privacy, the therapist's presence typically serves as the feared stimulus to trigger the client's fear. Second, most clients have had a full medical workup before arriving at a mental health professional's office. If there is any evidence of difficulty urinating at home or alone and a medical evaluation has not been conducted, this should be done prior to starting treatment. Third, for obvious reasons, in-session exposures are actually *in vivo* exposures in the lavatory. The urge to urinate may be manipulated by having the client drink liquids prior to session.

Homework for *In Vivo* Exposure for Specific Social Phobias

Developing homework assignments for *in vivo* exposure can require substantial creativity. Pages 187–191 in the workbook provide extensive lists of suggestions. Because the situations are often so brief, it may be necessary to assign a greater number of exposures per week than is true for other types of fears.

Typical Course of In-Session and Homework Exposures

Next we will outline a typical course of exposures for a client of moderate severity using fear of writing in public as the example. Fewer or additional exposures can be conducted, depending upon the severity of the client's fears and progress in treatment. Consideration must also be given to the dimensions that make the situation more and less anxiety provoking. For this example, greater anxiety is related to writing the client's name. Homework for *in vivo* exposures is also described. However, very often clients have particular life circumstances (e.g., an out-of-town business trip) that offer excellent opportunities for exposure. These should be incorporated into homework whenever possible.

Exposure #1: Writing a sentence repeatedly on a sheet of paper with the therapist sitting a comfortable distance away but able to see whether the client's hand is shaking. Homework: Complete BYOCT Worksheet and write a brief letter in a moderately busy coffee shop three times during the coming week.

Exposure #2: Signing name repeatedly with the therapist sitting nearby to see whether the client's hand is shaking. Therapist indicates that they will examine the signatures together after the exposure. Homework: Make several small purchases during the week with a credit card in a nonthreatening, nonbusy store. Sign credit card receipt in front of clerk each time.

Exposure #3: Writing name repeatedly on the board in full view of the therapist. Homework: Make several small purchases during the week with a credit card at a threatening and/or busy store. Sign credit receipt in front of clerk and other people in line. Look for any opportunities to write extensively in front of others such as in-store credit applications (the client need not submit application or can close account later), slips for drawings, surveys, taking notes at work meetings, and so forth.

Exposure #4: Incorporate feared outcome by signing name repeatedly in front of the therapist while making hand shake on purpose. Write check in front of clinic receptionist while making hand shake slightly on purpose (check must still be legible). Homework: Make small purchase at busiest grocery store at busiest time every day. Write a check for purchase and do not get out checkbook until clerk has completely rung up the sale. Write check in full view of impatient customers in line and clerk.

As noted earlier, not every session needs to include an in-session exposure, so these four suggested exposures could happen over five or more sessions. Sessions without in-session exposures would focus on cognitive restructuring. Homework for nonexposure sessions would consist of *in vivo* exposures of increasing difficulty and that logically fall between the in-session exposures.

Chapter 15

Exposure and Cognitive Restructuring: Public Speaking Fears

(Corresponds to chapter 11 of the workbook)

Timeline

Variable

Materials Needed

- Copy of client workbook

- Dry erase board

- Social Anxiety Session Change Index (SASCI)

- Weekly Social Anxiety Session Change Graph (same copy as used last session)

- Table 5.1 (List of Thinking Errors)

- Figure 6.1 (Disputing Questions)

- Form for Recording Key Information During In-Session Exposures That Can Serve as Session Progress Note

- Worksheet 7.1 (Be Your Own Cognitive Therapist (BYOCT) Worksheet)

- Worksheet 12.1 (Peeling Your Onion—Discovering and Challenging Your Core Beliefs)

Session Outline

- Administer, score, and graph the SASCI

- Review homework

- Briefly review psychoeducation on public speaking anxiety

- Do in-session cognitive restructuring and exposure

- Assign homework

Homework

- Have the client complete exposure homework including Worksheet 7.1 (Be Your Own Cognitive Therapist (BYOCT) Worksheet).

- Instruct the client to continue small daily assignments.

- Instruct the client to read chapter 12 of the workbook, if the client is ready for advanced cognitive restructuring.

- Have the client complete Worksheet 12.1 (Peeling Your Onion—Discovering and Challenging Your Core Beliefs)

Psychoeducation

Although chapter 11 of the workbook focuses on public speaking fears, many similar issues arise for any client who fears being the center of attention or speaking up in large or small groups such as meetings and classes. A sample of such situations appears in the self-assessment list on pages 193–194 of the workbook.

Most socially anxious individuals fear public speaking (Holt, Heimberg, Hope, & Liebowitz, 1992) but not all desire treatment for the problem. Individuals with more generalized fears may focus their treatment goals on making conversations, dating, or being assertive as these fears may have greater impact on their lives. On the other hand, some individuals seek treatment for anxiety about presentations and have little difficulty with other situations. Although such fears may be long-standing, individuals with public speaking anxiety are often prompted to seek treatment by a new opportunity, such as a promotion at work, or following what they perceive to be a failed public speaking experience.

Public speaking situations vary greatly in their demands. Speaking up in class or running an informal meeting may require little expertise or polished skills. Formal speeches can be much more demanding, and the therapist will need to understand what quality of performance is acceptable in the setting. This can be challenging as the client very often has perfectionistic standards that may not match reality. Chapter 11 of the workbook contains examples of clients facing situations with greater and lesser demands.

Designing In-Session Exposures

The largest difficulty in designing in-session exposures for individuals with fears about public speaking is being able to create the conditions that will evoke anxiety. Individuals with more severe or more generalized fears of speaking in groups or being the center of attention may initially respond to in-session role plays such as telling a personal story or reading in front of the therapist. In very rare cases, if the fear is circumscribed to a specific setting or large audience, then in-session work may need to rely on imaginal exposure. In-session exposures designed to be as challenging as possible (e.g., unfriendly audience, several unfamiliar role players, difficult questions) should be attempted prior to moving to imaginal exposures to ensure that the client is not discounting how anxiety-provoking an in-session exposure may be.

In imaginal exposure, the therapist uses guided imagery to expose the client to feared situations. Cognitive restructuring can occur before and after, as with role-played exposure. Typically, the therapist makes an audio recording of the exposure for the client to listen to repeatedly as homework. Imaginal exposure is most effective if it fully elicits the feared schema and triggers emotional processing (Foa & Kozak, 1986). Incorporating cues for all three components of anxiety—physiological, behavioral, and cognitive—as well as cues for all senses—the feel of the wood of the lectern, the sounds of the audience—is very important. Imaginal scenarios may run from 10 to 15 min, including a minute or two of relaxed breathing as the client settles into a chair or recliner at the beginning of the scenario and to close out the exposure. Because imaginal exposure is less intense than role-played or *in vivo* exposure, more challenging situations can be faced earlier in treatment.

Ideally, for role-played exposures of public speaking, the therapist will be able to assemble a few people to serve as audience members. This works well in group treatment but is more difficult in some clinical settings and individual treatment. Using a lectern and arranging the chairs to simulate an audience may be helpful even if the audience fails to fill the chairs. Whether or not an audience is available, two other strategies can cue evaluative fears. The presence of a video camera often triggers anxiety and may substitute for an audience (and may also be used for video feedback). Moving to a formal setting may also be helpful. Even if the therapist is the only person in the audience, speaking in a formal auditorium or conference room may help simulate the feared situation. The client may have access to an appropriate setting or the therapist can find one. Colleges and universities may be open to the public or available upon request when no other activities are scheduled. Community centers or religious institutions may have an appropriate room that they are willing to let someone use during off-hours. The therapist can make arrangements to meet the client at the location, taking appropriate precautions to guard confidentiality. With the client's permission, it is usually sufficient to say that someone has an important speech coming up and they want to practice. Because most people have some public speaking anxiety, this explanation typically generates few questions.

In addition to situational cues, the difficulty of the public speaking exposure can be manipulated by using the dimensions that underlie a client's fear. Typically these include amount of preparation, questions or other challenges from the audience, reading versus speaking spontaneously, or the extensiveness of the client's notes. Some of these dimensions also incorporate feared outcomes into the exposure.

Strategies for Cognitive Restructuring

Chapter 11 of the workbook describes many of the common automatic thoughts (ATs) reported by individuals with public speaking fears. These usually center on the visibility of anxiety symptoms or concerns about the quality of one's performance. For both types of ATs, postexposure ratings (as described in chapter 12 of this therapist guide) are often very helpful.

Often one of the primary purposes of public speaking is to communicate information. ATs may center on whether the audience understood the information or whether it was covered clearly or completely. The client can test this hypothesis by quizzing the audience on the content of the speech as part of postexposure debriefing. This can be quite powerful because it is difficult for audience members, including the therapist, to fake knowledge. If possible, audience members should be informed ahead of time about a possible knowledge test so they pay adequate attention. If the content is complex or the client sets perfectionistic standards, the therapist may want to agree upon a passing grade for the audience in advance.

Homework for *In Vivo* Exposure

Individuals with fears of public speaking may seek treatment because they need to do it regularly. This facilitates homework assignments because there are multiple opportunities for *in vivo* exposure. Often, however, the therapist will need to assist the client in seeking out additional opportunities. The most difficult case to treat is the client who needs assistance with a large event that occurs very infrequently. Intervention with such a case is described on pages 202–205 of the workbook.

Finding Opportunities for Being the Center of Attention

Any opportunity in which the client is the center of attention may trigger social anxiety and serve as a useful exposure for individuals with presentation fears. For example, leaving the center seat in a crowded movie theater and/or walking across the front may be a helpful exposure. Clients may have to seek out opportunities by joining an organization, attending a lecture, or taking a class. Some homework exposures we have used include:

- Asking a question or making a statement in a class or community meeting

- Volunteering to do a reading or prayer for a religious service

- Volunteering to take a turn leading a small group such as a book discussion group or religious class

- Joining a community sports team such as softball or bowling

- Preparing testimony on an issue and giving it at a public hearing such as a city council or county board

- Taking a public speaking course

- Joining Toastmasters International, a public speaking organization available in many communities

Typical Course of In-Session and *In Vivo* Exposures

The course of treatment should be highly individualized, but below we present a typical course for someone seeking help with anxiety about speaking at meetings and who occasionally needs to make informal presentations.

Exposure #1: Sitting in front of the therapist and spontaneously speaking about a familiar topic. Homework: At least once during the week, tell a personal story in a group of people when the client would normally remain silent.

Exposure #2: Standing in front of the therapist and reading from an unfamiliar book or magazine, perhaps with technical vocabulary the client may not know. Homework: At least three times during the week, briefly speak up in a group or at a meeting when the client normally would remain silent. Begin developing opportunities to practice being the center of attention or speaking, such as joining a group or arranging an upcoming speaking opportunity.

Exposure #3: Standing in front of the therapist giving a prepared or unprepared speech with or without notes. Homework: If possible, make a brief presentation in a reasonably safe setting. Otherwise, continue speaking up in groups or meetings more frequently and for longer.

Exposure #4: Speaking in front of the therapist (with other audience members if possible) in a formal setting such as a conference room or auditorium. Homework: Make a brief presentation of some type. This could be an informal presentation such as making a somewhat extended point (2 to 3 min minimum) at a community meeting. Continue daily or near-daily opportunities to speak briefly in a group or meeting.

Exposure #5: A prepared speech in a formal setting with the therapist (and other audience members if possible) that incorporates a feared outcome such as losing notes or hostile questions from the audience. Homework: Make a more formal or extended presentation as opportunity arises in daily life or via created opportunity, such as giving testimony at a public hearing.

As noted earlier, not every session includes an in-session exposure, so these five suggested exposures could happen over six or more sessions. Sessions without in-session exposures would focus on cognitive restructuring and problem solving getting involved in opportunities for speaking. Homework for nonexposure sessions would be *in vivo* exposures that are of increasing difficulty and logically fall between the in-session exposures.

Chapter 16 | *Advanced Cognitive Restructuring*

(Corresponds to chapter 12 of the workbook)

Timeline

One to two sessions initially; then additional sessions as needed to challenge core belief

Materials Needed

- Copy of client workbook

- Dry erase board

- Social Anxiety Session Change Index (SASCI)

- Weekly Social Anxiety Session Change Graph (same copy as used last session)

- Client's completed BYOCT Worksheets

- Table 5.1 (List of Thinking Errors)

- Figure 6.1 (Disputing Questions)

- Form for Recording Key Information During In-Session Exposures That Can Serve as Session Progress Note

- Worksheet 7.1 (Be Your Own Cognitive Therapist (BYOCT) Worksheet)

- Worksheet 12.1 (Peeling Your Onion—Discovering and Challenging Your Core Beliefs)

Session Outline

- Review, score, and graph SASCI

- Review homework

- Explain rationale behind advanced cognitive restructuring

- Review case vignettes regarding core beliefs

- Conduct Peeling Your Onion—Discovering and Challenging Your Core Beliefs exercise (Worksheet 12.1 in the workbook)

- Assign homework

Homework

- Have the client complete exposure homework to test core belief.

- Instruct the client to continue small daily assignments.

Overview

As usual, the session begins with review of the SASCI, a discussion of homework from the previous session, and agenda setting. Chapter 12 of the workbook is titled "Advanced Cognitive Restructuring: Addressing Core Beliefs." As individuals work through various exposures and associated cognitive restructuring, both the therapist and the client often notice that certain themes keep reoccurring. According to Persons (1989; 2008), effective cognitive therapy eventually needs to address underlying core beliefs for lasting change to occur. Themes in automatic thoughts (ATs) reflect a core belief that drives all of the difficulties the person is experiencing. Persons calls this approach "Case Formulation" and suggests numerous strategies to identify core beliefs. The client workbook relies on a common cognitive strategy for moving beyond more superficial ATs called the "downward arrow" technique (J. S. Beck, 1995), based on the analogy of peeling away the layers of an onion (see Worksheet 12.1 in the client workbook).

As noted previously, over the course of therapy, cognitive restructuring should move from more superficial to more important or core beliefs. These more core beliefs may not come to mind as easily, they are often associated with heightened affect, and the client may be more reluctant to discuss them. Once the client makes some significant improvement as assessed by the SASCI and BYOCT Worksheets and completes at least three to four exposures, and the therapist sees that cognitive restructuring frequently returns to a common theme, then it is time to work through chapter 12 of the workbook. In most cases, this is sometime after session 12. This does not signal the end of exposure; rather, it helps focus what subsequent exposures and cognitive restructuring should accomplish.

Identifying Core Beliefs

According to Persons, the case formulation reflects a unifying statement that can be used to explain all of the presenting problems. These statements reflect underlying beliefs about the person, the way the world works, or what to expect from other people. Examples of core beliefs include "I must always be perfect," "The world is not fair," and "If people really knew me, they would not like me." The client and the therapist can move from more superficial ATs to the core belief by following the meaning and implications of the ATs as is done on Worksheet 12.1. However, the therapist should not limit himself or herself to the strategies on the worksheet. This is just the starting point for more careful and thorough work that may extend over a couple of sessions. Because clients may have more difficulty discussing core beliefs, we often find it helpful to provide the clients with a strong rationale for exploring core beliefs.

Additionally, if the therapist suspects that the client may be resistant to discussing core beliefs, he or she should first review with the client the case vignettes regarding core beliefs found in chapter 12 of the workbook. Therapists should use a combination of Socratic questioning and active listening skills to explore the meaning of ATs and the associated affect. The disputing questions may be used to explore the meaning of an AT, but it is often useful to allow the client to experience and describe the affective experience associated with the answer to the disputing questions. This effect may trigger important memories or other ATs that can then be explored further. Another technique to uncover core beliefs is to unpack the meaning of emotionally loaded words like "perfect," "right," "best," "never," and "should."

There are several signs an AT reflects a core belief. Core beliefs are often long-standing beliefs that seem fundamentally true to the person. Very often, they were true in the past or were the views communicated by influential people such as parents. The core belief should explain why the client experiences social anxiety in the range of situations she does as well as the dimensions identified in the Fear and Avoidance Hierarchy.

Once the therapist believes the core belief has been identified, then he or she should share it with the client, including his or her understanding of how it explains the client's social anxiety. Persons (1989, 2008) identifies several tests to determine whether one is on the right track with such a formulation. These are adapted for the current treatment. First, the formulation should make sense and explain most aspects of the client's social anxiety. Second, the client should recognize the formulation as true. This may be an "a-ha" experience for the client. Third, the formulation should identify the nature of future exposures. Fourth, the formulation should lead to effective intervention.

The examples of core beliefs in the workbook reflect quite dramatic presentations that are not initially obvious from the ATs. This is not always the case, especially for individuals with more circumscribed fears or who may be earlier in the course of the disorder. For public speaking anxiety, the core belief may be that a previous bad speaking experience will be repeated. The client may not have catastrophic interpretations of another bad experience but simply fear the discomfort and immediate social consequences.

Core Beliefs Are Not Simply Insight and Should Be Directly Challenged

Therapists trained in insight-oriented therapy often confuse identification of core beliefs with client insight. Understanding the core belief may help the client understand more about her social anxiety and how to overcome it. However, identification of the core belief is only useful if it directs what cognitive and behavioral changes need to occur. Unless the client gathers evidence to challenge the core belief, there is little reason to think it will change. Thus, the core belief helps the therapist and the client focus on what types of schema-discrepant information need to be processed by the client to establish lasting behavioral change and symptom reduction. The core belief is challenged by cognitive restructuring and exposure. This is the primary focus for the remainder of treatment.

Chapter 17 *Termination*

(Corresponds to chapter 13 of the workbook)

Timeline

One session; may be extended to two sessions if discussion of progress reveals need for further intervention

Materials Needed

■ Copy of client workbook

■ Social Anxiety Session Change Index (SASCI)

■ Weekly Social Anxiety Session Change Graph (same copy as used last session)

■ Client's completed BYOCT Worksheets

■ Table 5.1 (List of Thinking Errors)

■ Figure 6.1 (Disputing Questions)

■ Form for Recording Key Information During In-Session Exposures That Can Serve as Session Progress Note

■ Worksheet 7.1 (Be Your Own Cognitive Therapist (BYOCT) Worksheet)

Session Outline

- Review, score, and graph SASCI

- Assess progress

- Make decisions about additional treatment

- Discuss relapse prevention

- Explain termination procedure

- What to expect after treatment

- When to call for a booster session

- Acknowledgment of mixed emotions of leaving therapy

Overview

Chapter 13 in the client workbook focuses on assessment of progress, relapse prevention, and termination. After approximately 15 sessions of treatment for the typical client with moderately severe symptoms, it is time to stop and assess progress. Treatment for social anxiety may continue with the same interventions, additional interventions may be added, all treatment may end, or treatment may shift to focus on other issues.

Assessing Progress

Progress assessment involves reviewing the progress checklist on page 223 in the workbook and re-rating the Fear and Avoidance Hierarchy. It is normal for some social anxiety to remain, but the avoidance ratings should be dramatically reduced. Typically, avoidance behavior decreases first, followed by decreases in fear. If avoidance is not approaching zero for many of the hierarchy situations and/or fear ratings remain above 50 for items important to the treatment goals, then additional intervention is probably appropriate.

Even if progress has not been as rapid or complete as hoped, nearly all clients have made some progress at this point. The therapist should help the client take credit for the progress and identify the thinking error of disqualifying the positive as it arises. One advantage of psychosocial interventions over medication is that the client can take full credit for change because of his hard work.

Decisions About Additional Treatment

More of the Same

If the treatment seems to be working (i.e., if the client appears to be fully engaged in the intervention and fear and avoidance are decreasing), then additional sessions of cognitive restructuring and exposure, especially focused on the core belief, are recommended. In-session exposures may be infrequent because the primary emphasis is on making changes in the client's daily life. The assessment of progress should be repeated as appropriate.

Adding Interventions

If the client seems to be making some progress but is having difficulty fully engaging in exposure because of excessive anxiety, then it may be appropriate to add additional interventions. These could include medication or additional anxiety management strategies such as applied muscle relaxation or diaphragmatic breathing. Once the anxiety is more under control, the client should be able to more fully engage in in-session and *in vivo* exposure and cognitive restructuring. The assessment of progress should be repeated as appropriate.

Stopping Treatment for Social Anxiety

Our research protocols are 12 sessions for group treatment and 16 sessions over 20 weeks for individual treatment. For most individuals with social anxiety, this duration seems sufficient to launch them on a new path of reduced anxiety and avoidance. Individuals with more generalized fears may require additional sessions. Regardless of whether treatment stops at the first assessment of progress or after additional treatment, some anxiety will likely remain. However, the client should feel reasonably confident about continuing to face the remaining fears on his own. The cognitive coping skills are firmly in place to handle anxiety that arises as new situations are encountered. The attitude that anxiety is a cue to face, not avoid, fears is firmly established. If the decision is made to stop treatment, then the material on relapse prevention in chapter 13 of the client workbook should be thoroughly covered. This typically requires one-half to one session. Stopping or fading treatment for social anxiety does not mean that sessions are necessarily terminated. Our research suggests that comorbid conditions such as depression typically improve with treatment of social anxiety. Occasionally, however, the client has additional concerns that should now be the focus of intervention.

Relapse Prevention

As treatment for social anxiety winds down, clients may be quite vulnerable to relapse as they leave the ongoing support and structure of therapy. Research in other areas such as substance abuse (Marlatt & Gordon, 1985) has indicated that incorporating relapse prevention strategies helps maintain treatment gains. The client workbook includes several relapse prevention techniques including strategies to establish ongoing change, and instructions about when to return for booster sessions.

For some clients, therapists may have noticed that there are individuals or circumstances in their lives that are encouraging a return to previous behavior patterns. This may be a family member who is more accustomed to an anxious and avoiding person and, purposefully or not, reinforces problematic behaviors. Although most therapists may recognize that the tendency toward homeostasis in families and broader social networks may encourage relapse, this notion is novel to most clients. Identifying where such pressures may lie can be helpful as the client attempts to establish a new behavior pattern of approach to previously feared situations. It is encouraging that once the new pattern is established, the same homeostasis may help maintain it.

One of the primary reasons we emphasize that clients learn to use cognitive restructuring skills on their own, as well as with the therapist assistance in session, is that these skills are broadly useful in life. Having the cognitive skills available should help the client handle inevitable new anxiety-provoking situations as well as other life stressors. The client should also be able to identify Thinking Errors related to his continued progress, such as Disqualifying the Positive when successes occur and Catastrophizing when setbacks occur.

In our experience, clients inevitably take a brief respite from facing challenging situations in the first couple of weeks after therapy. Without the structure of weekly homework, they may not consistently seek out new situations. We counter this tendency by asking them to set a goal for one month after treatment. We encourage them to enter this goal on their calendar as a reminder to get back on track for maintaining progress and continuing to conquer social anxiety.

Termination

The client workbook also covers the usual termination issues, including what to expect following treatment, how to know when to call the therapist for a booster session, and acknowledging one's mixed emotions about leaving therapy. In group treatment, we end the final session with soft drinks and snacks to allow the group time to say good-bye and assist in the transition to the end of therapy.

Only a small number of clients seek booster sessions, and many of these can be handled over the phone. Most commonly, individuals who do well in treatment see continued progress. Booster sessions tend to occur only when some new circumstances elicit substantial increases in anxiety.

Socially anxious individuals, especially those who have been very isolated, may become quite attached to the therapist. The strong bond can be helpful during treatment, as the client needs to trust the therapist to engage in exposure and disclose about automatic thoughts. When terminating treatment, however, the therapist should be sure to attend sufficiently to this attachment. It may help to view termination as a time of celebration of the client's accomplishments. In fact, we often refer to termination as "graduation." The therapist should express positive feelings about having worked with the client and his accomplishments. It may also be helpful to model that it is acceptable to experience some sadness at the end of therapy.

Appendix of Assessment Measures

SIAS

_____ 1. I get nervous if I have to speak with someone in authority (teacher, boss).

_____ 2. I have difficulty making eye-contact with others.

_____ 3. I become tense if I have to talk about myself or my feelings.

_____ 4. I find it difficult mixing comfortably with the people I work with.

_____ 5. I find it easy to make friends of my own age.

_____ 6. I tense-up if I meet an acquaintance in the street.

_____ 7. When mixing socially, I am uncomfortable.

_____ 8. I feel tense if I am alone with just one person.

_____ 9. I am at ease meeting people at parties, etc.

_____ 10. I have difficulty talking with other people.

_____ 11. I find it easy to think of things to talk about.

_____ 12. I worry about expressing myself in case I appear awkward.

_____ 13. I find it difficult to disagree with another's point of view.

_____ 14. I have difficulty talking to attractive persons of the opposite sex.

_____ 15. I find myself worrying that I won't know what to say in social situations.

_____ 16. I am nervous mixing with people I don't know well.

_____ 17. I feel I'll say something embarrassing when talking.

_____ 18. When mixing in a group, I find myself worrying I will be ignored.

_____ 19. I am tense mixing in a group.

_____ 20. I am unsure whether to greet someone I know only slightly.

The Social Interaction Anxiety Scale (SIAS). Reprinted with the permission of Richard P. Mattick.

SPS

_____ 1. I become anxious if I have to write in front of other people.

_____ 2. I become self-conscious when using public toilets.

_____ 3. I can suddenly become aware of my own voice and of others listening to me.

_____ 4. I get nervous that people are staring at me as I walk down the street.

_____ 5. I fear I may blush when I am with others.

_____ 6. I feel self-conscious if I have to enter a room where others are already seated.

_____ 7. I worry about shaking or trembling when I'm watched by other people.

_____ 8. I would get tense if I had to sit facing other people on a bus or a train.

_____ 9. I get panicky that others might see me faint or be sick or ill.

_____ 10. I would find it difficult to drink something if in a group of people.

_____ 11. It would make me feel self-conscious to eat in front of a stranger at a restaurant.

_____ 12. I am worried people will think my behavior odd.

_____ 13. I would get tense if I had to carry a tray across a crowded cafeteria.

_____ 14. I worry I'll lose control of myself in front of other people.

_____ 15. I worry I might do something to attract the attention of other people.

_____ 16. When in an elevator, I am tense if people look at me.

_____ 17. I can feel conspicuous standing in a line.

_____ 18. I can get tense when I speak in front of other people.

_____ 19. I worry my head will shake or nod in front of others.

_____ 20. I feel awkward and tense if I know people are watching me.

The Social Phobia Scale (SPS). Reprinted with the permission of Richard P. Mattick.

BFNE

Read each of the following statements carefully and indicate how characteristic it is of you according to the following scale.

1 = Not at all characteristic of me
2 = Slightly characteristic of me
3 = Moderately characteristic of me
4 = Very characteristic of me
5 = Extremely characteristic of me

_____ 1. I worry about what other people will think of me even when I know it doesn't make a difference.

_____ 2. I am unconcerned even if I know people are forming an unfavorable impression of me.

_____ 3. I am frequently afraid of other people noticing my shortcomings.

_____ 4. I rarely worry about what kind of impression I am making on someone.

_____ 5. I am afraid that others will not approve of me.

_____ 6. I am afraid that people will find fault with me.

_____ 7. Other people's opinions of me do not bother me.

_____ 8. When I am talking to someone, I worry about what they may be thinking about me.

_____ 9. I am usually worried about what kind of impression I make.

_____ 10. If I know someone is judging me, it has little effect on me.

_____ 11. Sometimes I think I am too concerned with what other people think of me.

_____ 12. I often worry that I will say or do the wrong things.

The Brief Fear of Negative Evaluation Scale (BFNE). Reprinted from Leary, M. R. (1983). A brief version of the Fear of Negative Evaluation Scale. *Personality and Social Psychology Bulletin, 9*, 373. Copyright © 1983 by Society for Personality and Social Psychology. Reprinted by permission of Sage Publications. All rights reserved.

LSAS

This measure assesses the way that social phobia plays a role in your life across a variety of situations. Read each situation carefully and answer two questions about that situation. The first question asks how anxious or fearful you feel in the situation. The second question asks how often you avoid the situation. If you come across a situation that you ordinarily do not experience, we ask that you imagine "what if you were faced with that situation," and then, rate the degree to which you would fear this hypothetical situation and how often you would tend to avoid it. Please base your ratings on the way that the situations have affected you in the last week. *Fill out the following scale with the most suitable answer provided below.*

Fear or Anxiety	Avoidance
0 = None	0 = Never (0%)
1 = Mild	1 = Occasionally (1%–33%)
2 = Moderate	2 = Often (33%–67%)
3 = Severe	3 = Usually (67%–100%)

Fear and avoidance ratings scales for use by the client during clinician administration of Liebowitz Social Anxiety Scale. This scale is copyrighted and may not be reproduced without the permission of the copyright holder, Michael R. Liebowitz, M. D., who can be reached at MRL1945@aol.com or (212) 543-5370.

	Fear (S)	Fear (P)	Avoidance (S)	Avoidance (P)
1. Telephoning in public				
2. Participating in small groups				
3. Eating in public places				
4. Drinking with others in public places				
5. Talking to people in authority				
6. Acting, performing, or giving a talk in front of an audience				
7. Going to a party				
8. Working while being observed				
9. Writing while being observed				
10. Calling someone you don't know very well				
11. Talking with people you don't know very Well				

	Fear (S)	Fear (P)	Avoidance (S)	Avoidance (P)
12. Meeting strangers				
13. Urinating in a public bathroom				
14. Entering a room when others are already seated				
15. Being the center of attention				
16. Speaking up at a meeting				
17. Taking a test				
18. Expressing a disagreement or disapproval to people you don't know very well				

	Fear		Avoidance	
	(S)	(P)	(S)	(P)
19. Looking at people you don't know very Well in the eyes				
20. Giving a report to a group				
21. Trying to pick up someone				
22. Returning goods to a store				
23. Giving a party				
24. Resisting a high pressure salesperson				
Performance Subscales				
Social Interaction Subscales				
Total Fear Subscale				
Total Avoidance Subscale				
TOTAL SCORE				

Table A.1 Scoring Instructions for Social Anxiety Instruments

Instrument	Scoring Instructions
Social Interaction Anxiety Scale (SIAS)	Reverse-score items 5, 9, and 11, and then sum items 1–20.
Social Phobia Scale (SPS)	Sum items 1–20.
Brief Fear of Negative Evaluation Scale (BFNE)	Reverse-score items 2, 4, 7, and 10, and then sum all items.
Liebowitz Social Anxiety Scale (LSAS)	
Fear of social interaction	Sum social (S) fear items 5, 7, 10, 11, 12, 15, 18, 19, 22, 23, and 24.
Avoidance of social interaction	Sum social (S) avoidance items 5, 7, 10, 11, 12, 15, 18, 19, 22, 23, and 24.
Fear of performance	Sum performance (P) fear items 1, 2, 3, 4, 6, 8, 9, 13, 14, 16, 17, 20, and 21.
Avoidance of performance	Sum performance (P) avoidance items 1, 2, 3, 4, 6, 8, 9, 13, 14, 16, 17, 20, and 21.
Total Fear	Sum social (S) fear and performance (P) fear items 1 through 24.
Total Avoidance	Sum social (S) avoidance and performance (P) avoidance items 1 through 24.
Total Score	Sum the total fear subscale and the total avoidance subscale.

Table A.2 Means, Standard Deviations, and Suggested Cut-Off Scores Derived from Samples of Clients with Social Anxiety Disorder and Community Controls on Measures of Social Anxiety

Instrument	Range	Means (Standard Deviations)		Suggested Cut-Off Scores	
		Clients[1]	Controls[2]	Social Anxiety Disorder[3]	Generalized Subtype[4]
Social Interaction Anxiety Scale	0–80	49.0 (15.6)	19.9 (14.2)	34	42
Social Phobia Scale	0–80	32.8 (14.8)	12.5 (11.5)	24	—
Brief Fear of Negative Evaluation Scale	12–60	46.1 (9.5)	26.2 (5.1)	—	—
Liebowitz Social Anxiety Scale					
Fear of social interaction	0–33	16.9 (7.7)	3.1 (3.0)	—	—
Avoidance of social interaction	0–33	15.7 (8.2)	3.1 (3.5)	—	—
Fear of performance	0–39	18.6 (6.8)	3.8 (3.3)	—	—
Avoidance of performance	0–39	16.0 (7.3)	3.6 (3.3)	—	—
Total Fear	0–72	35.5 (13.6)	6.9 (5.8)	—	—
Total Avoidance	0–72	31.6 (14.5)	6.7 (6.0)	—	—
Total Score	0–144	67.2 (27.5)	13.6 (11.1)	30	60

Notes: Information provided for the Liebowitz Social Anxiety Scale (LSAS) was derived from the clinician-administered version of the scale.

[1] Social Interaction Anxiety Scale (SIAS) and Social Phobia Scale (SPS) data are from Heimberg, R. G., Mueller, G. P., Holt, C. S., Hope, D. A., & Leibowitz, M. R. (1992). Assessment of anxiety in social interaction and being observed by others: The Social Interaction Anxiety Scale and the Social Phobia Scale. *Behavior Therapy, 23*, 53–73. Brief Fear of Negative Evaluation (BFNE) Scale data are from Weeks J. W., Heimberg, R. G., Fresco, D. M., Hart, T. A., Turk, C. L., Schnieier, F. R., et al. (2005). Empirical validation and psychometric evaluation of the Brief Fear of Negative Evaluation Scale in patients with social anxiety disorder. *Psychological Assessment, 17*, 179–190; LSAS data are from Heimberg, R. G., Horner, K. J., Juster, H. R., Safren, S.A., Brown, E. J., Schneier, F. R., et al. (1999). Psychometric properties of the Liebowitz Social Anxiety Scale. *Psychological Medicine, 29*, 199–212.

[2] SIAS and SPS data are from Heimberg, R. G., Mueller, G. P., Holt, C. S., Hope, D. A., & Leibowitz, M. R. (1992). Assessment of anxiety in social interaction and being observed by others: The Social Interaction Anxiety Scale and the Social Phobia Scale. *Behavior Therapy, 23*, 53–73. BFNE data are from Weeks et al. (2005); LSAS data are from Heimberg, R. G., Horner, K. J., Juster, H. R., Safren, S. A., Brown, E. J., Schneier, F. R., et al. (1999). Psychometric properties of the Liebowitz Social Anxiety Scale. *Psychological Medicine, 29*, 199–212.

[3] SIAS and SPS data are from Heimberg, R. G., Mueller, G. P., Holt, C. S., Hope, D. A., & Leibowitz, M. R. (1992). Assessment of anxiety in social interaction and being observed by others: The Social Interaction Anxiety Scale and the Social Phobia Scale. *Behavior Therapy, 23*, 53–73. LSAS Total Score data are from Mennin, D. S., Fresco, D. M., Heimberg, R. G., Schneier, F. R., Davies, S. O., & Liebowitz, M. R. (2002). Screening for social anxiety disorder in the clinical setting: Using the Liebowitz Social Anxiety Scale. *Journal of Anxiety Disorders, 16*, 661–673.

[4] SIAS data are from Mennin, D. S., Fresco, D. M., & Heimberg, R. G., (1998, November). *Determining subtype of social phobia in session: Validation using a receiver operating characteristic (ROC) analysis.* Paper presented at the 32nd annual meeting of the Association for Advancement of Behavior Therapy, Washington, DC. LSAS Total Score data are from Mennin, D. S., Fresco, D. M., Heimberg, R. G., Schneier, F. R., Davies, S. O., & Liebowitz, M. R. (2002). Screening for social anxiety disorder in the clinical setting: Using the Liebowitz Social Anxiety Scale. *Journal of Anxiety Disorders, 16*, 661–673.

References

Abbott, M. J., & Rapee, R. M. (2004). Post-event rumination and negative self-appraisal in social phobia before and after treatment. *Journal of Abnormal Psychology, 113*, 136–144.

Acarturk, C., Cuijpers, P., van Straten, A., & de Graaf, R. (2009). Psychological treatment of social anxiety disorder: A meta-analysis. *Psychological Medicine, 39*, 241–254.

Alden, L. E., & Wallace, S. T. (1995). Social phobia and social appraisal in successful and unsuccessful social interactions. *Behaviour Research and Therapy, 33*, 497–505.

American Psychiatric Association. (1980). *Diagnostic and statistical manual of mental disorders* (3rd ed.). Washington, DC: Author.

American Psychiatric Association. (1987). *Diagnostic and statistical manual of mental disorders* (3rd ed., revised). Washington, DC: Author.

American Psychiatric Association. (1994). *Diagnostic and statistical manual of mental disorders* (4th ed.). Washington, DC: Author.

American Psychiatric Association. (2000). *Diagnostic and statistical manual of mental disorders* (4th ed., text revision). Washington, DC: Author.

Arkowitz, H., & Westra, H. (2004). Integrating motivational interviewing and cognitive behavior therapy in the treatment of depression and anxiety. *Journal of Cognitive Psychotherapy: An International Quarterly, 18*, 337–349.

Asmundson, G. J. G., & Stein, M. B. (1994). Selective attention for social threat in patients with generalized social phobia: Evaluation using a dot-probe paradigm. *Journal of Anxiety Disorders, 8*, 107–117.

Beck, J. S. (1995). *Cognitive therapy: Basics and beyond.* New York: Guilford Press.

Beck, A. T., Steer, R. A., & Brown, G. K. (1996). *Beck Depression Inventory manual* (2nd ed.). San Antonio: The Psychological Corporation.

Blackmore, M., Erwin, B. A., Heimberg, R. G., Magee, L., & Fresco, D. M. (2009). Social anxiety disorder and specific phobias. In M. G. Gelder,

J. J. Lopez-Ibor, N. C. Andreason, & J. Geddes (Eds.), *New oxford textbook of psychiatry* (2nd ed., Vol. 1, pp. 739–750). Oxford: Oxford University Press.

Blanco, C., Heimberg, R. G., Schneier, F. R., Fresco, D. M., Chen, H., Turk, C. L., et al. (2010). A placebo-controlled trial of phenelzine, cognitive behavioral group therapy and their combination for social anxiety disorder. *Archives of General Psychiatry, 67*, 286–295.

Borkovec, T. D., & Nau, S. D. (1972). Credibility of analogue therapy rationales. *Journal of Behavior Therapy and Experimental Psychiatry, 3*, 257–260.

Brown, E. J., Heimberg, R. G., & Juster, H. R. (1995). Social phobia subtype and avoidant personality disorder: Effect on severity of social phobia, impairment, and outcome of cognitive-behavioral treatment. *Behavior Therapy, 26*, 467–486.

Brown, E. J., Turovsky, J., Heimberg, R. G., Juster, H. R., Brown, T. A., & Barlow, D. H. (1997). Validation of the social interaction anxiety scale and the social phobia scale across the anxiety disorders. *Psychological Assessment, 9*, 21–27.

Brozovich, F., & Heimberg, R.G. (2008). An analysis of post-event processing in social anxiety disorder. *Clinical Psychology Review, 28*, 891–903.

Bruch, M. A., Gorsky, J. M., Collins, T. M., & Berger, P. (1989). Shyness and sociability reexamined: A multicomponent analysis. *Journal of Personality and Social Psychology, 57*, 904–915.

Chambless, D. L., Tran, G. Q., & Glass, C. R. (1997). Predictors of response to cognitive-behavioral group therapy for social phobia. *Journal of Anxiety Disorders, 11*, 221–240.

Chartier, M. J., Hazen, A. L., & Stein, M. B. (1998). Lifetime patterns of social phobia: A retrospective study of the course of social phobia in a nonclinical population. *Depression and Anxiety, 7*, 113–121.

Clark, D. M. (2001). A cognitive perspective on social phobia. In W. R. Crozier & L. E. Alden (Eds.), *International handbook of social anxiety: Concepts, research and interventions relating to the self and shyness* (pp. 405–430). New York: John Wiley & Sons.

Clark, D. M., & Wells, A. (1995). A cognitive model of social phobia. In R. Heimberg, M. Liebowitz, D. A. Hope, & F. R. Schneier (Eds.), *Social phobia: Diagnosis, assessment, and treatment* (pp. 69–93). New York: Guilford Press.

Coles, M. E., Turk, C. L., Heimberg, R. G., & Fresco, D. M. (2001). Effects of varying levels of anxiety within social situations: Relationship to memory perspective and attributions in social phobia. *Behaviour Research and Therapy, 39*, 651–665.

Connor, K. M., Davidson, J. R. T., Churchill, L. E., Sherwood, A., Foa, E., & Weisler, R. H. (2000). Psychometric properties of the Social Phobia Inventory (SPIN). *British Journal of Psychiatry, 176,* 379–386.

Connor, K. M., Kobak, K. A., Churchill, L. E., Katzelnick, D., & Davidson, J. R. T. (2001). Mini-SPIN: A brief screening assessment for generalized social anxiety disorder. *Depression and Anxiety, 14,* 137–140.

Cuming, S., Rapee, R. M., Kempa, N., Abbott, M. J., Peters, L., & Gaston, J. E. (2009). A self-report measure of subtle avoidance and safety behaviors relevant to social anxiety: Development and psychometric properties. *Journal of Anxiety Disorders, 23,* 879–883.

Dannahy, L., & Stopa, L. (2007). Post-event processing in social anxiety. *Behaviour Research and Therapy, 45,* 1207–1219.

Davidson, J. R. T., Foa, E. B., Huppert, J. D., Keefe, F. J., Franklin, M. E., Compton, J., et al. (2004). Fluoxetine, comprehensive cognitive behavioral therapy, and placebo in generalized social phobia. *Archives of General Psychiatry, 61,* 1005–1013.

Davidson, J. R. T., Potts, N. L. S., Richichi, E. A., Krishnan, R. R., Ford, S. M., Smith, R. D., et al. (1991). The brief social phobia scale. *Journal of Clinical Psychiatry, 52,* 48–51.

De Coteau, T., Anderson, J., & Hope, D. A. (2006). Adapting manualized treatments: Treating anxiety disorders among Native Americans. *Cognitive and Behavioral Practice, 13,* 304–309.

DiNardo, P. A., Brown, T. A., & Barlow, D. H. (1994). *Anxiety disorders interview schedule for DSM-IV: Lifetime version (ADIS-IV-L).* San Antonio, TX: Psychological Corporation.

DiNardo, P. A., O'Brien, G. T., Barlow, D. H., Waddell, M. T., & Blanchard, E. B. (1983). Reliability of DSM-III anxiety disorder categories using a new structured interview. *Archives of General Psychiatry, 40,* 1070–1074.

Edelman, R. E., & Chambless, D. L. (1995). Adherence during session and homework in cognitive-behavioral group treatment of social phobia. *Behaviour Research and Therapy, 33,* 573–577.

Edwards, S. L., Rapee, R., & Franklin, J. (2003). Post-event rumination and recall bias for social performance event in high and low socially anxious individuals. *Cognitive Therapy and Research, 27,* 603–617.

Emge, T. M., & Hope, D. A. (2010). Social anxiety disorder. In J. C. Thomas & M. Hersen (Eds.), *Handbook of clinical psychology competencies.* New York: Springer.

Erwin, B.A., Heimberg, R.G., Juster, H.R., & Mindlin, M. (2002). Comorbid anxiety and mood disorders among persons with social anxiety disorder. *Behaviour Research and Therapy, 40,* 19–35.

Fedoroff, I. C., & Taylor, S. (2001). Psychological and pharmacological treatments for social anxiety disorder: A meta-analysis. *Journal of Clinical Psychopharmacology, 21,* 311–324.

Feske, U., & Chambless, D. L. (1995). Cognitive behavioral versus exposure only treatment for social phobia: A meta-analysis. *Behavior Therapy, 26,* 295–720.

Feske, U., Perry, K. J., Chambless, D. L., Renneberg, B., & Goldstein, A. J. (1996). Avoidant personality disorder as a predictor for severity and treatment outcome among generalized social phobics. *Journal of Personality Disorders, 10,* 174–184.

First, M. B., Spitzer, R. L., Gibbon, M., & Williams, J. (2002). *Structured clinical interview for DSM-IV-TR axis I disorders—Patient edition (SCID-I/P).* New York, NY: Biometrics Research Department.

Foa, E. B., & Kozak, M. J. (1986). Emotional processing of fear: Exposure to corrective information. *Psychological Bulletin, 99,* 20–35.

Frank, J. D., & Frank, J. B. (1991). *Persuasion and healing: A comparative study of psychotherapy.* Baltimore: John Hopkins University Press.

Fresco, D. M., Coles, M. E., Heimberg, R. G., Liebowitz, M. R., Hami, S., Stein, M. B., et al. (2001). The Liebowitz Social Anxiety Scale: A comparison of the psychometric properties of self-report and clinician-administered formats. *Psychological Medicine, 31,* 1025–1035.

Frisch, M. B. (1994). *Manual and treatment guide for the Quality of Life Inventory.* Minneapolis, MN: National Computer Systems, Inc.

Gilbert, P. (2001). Evolution and social anxiety: The role of attraction, social competition, and social hierarchies. *Psychiatric Clinics of North America, 24,* 723–752.

Glasgow, R. E., & Arkowitz, H. (1975). The behavioral assessment of male and female social competence in dyadic interactions. *Behavior Therapy, 6,* 488–498.

Gould, R. A., Buckminster, S., Pollack, M. H., Otto, M. W., & Yap, L. (1997). Cognitive-behavioral and pharmacological treatment for social phobia: A meta-analysis. *Clinical Psychology: Science and Practice, 4,* 291–306.

Hackmann, A., Clark, D. M., & McManus, F. (2000). Recurrent images and early memories in social phobia. *Behaviour Research and Therapy, 38,* 601–610.

Hackmann, A., Surawy, C., & Clark, D. M. (1998). Seeing yourself through others' eyes: A study of spontaneously occurring images in social phobia. *Behavioural and Cognitive Psychotherapy, 26,* 3–12.

Halford, K., & Foddy, M. (1982). Cognitive and social skills correlates of social anxiety. *British Journal of Clinical Psychology, 21*, 17–28.

Hart, T. A., Jack, M. S., Turk, C. L., & Heimberg, R. G. (1999). Issues for the measurement of social anxiety disorder (social phobia). In H. G. M. Westenberg & J. A. Den Boer (Eds.), *Focus on psychiatry: Social anxiety disorder* (pp. 133–155). Amsterdam: Syn-Thesis Publishers.

Harvey, A. G., Clark, D. A., Ehlers, A., & Rapee, R. M. (2000). Social anxiety and self-impression: Cognitive preparation enhances the beneficial effects of video feedback following a stressful social task. *Behaviour Research and Therapy, 38*, 1183–1192.

Hayes, S. A., Hope, D. A., VanDyke, M., & Heimberg, R. G. (2007). Working alliance for clients with social anxiety disorder: Relationship with session helpfulness and within-session habituation. *Cognitive Behaviour Therapy, 36*, 34–42.

Hayes, S. A., Miller, N. A., Hope, D. A., Heimberg, R. G., & Juster, H. R. (2008). Assessing client progress session-by-session in the treatment of social anxiety disorder: The Social Anxiety Session Change Index. *Cognitive and Behavioral Practice, 15*, 203–211.

Hays, P. A., & Iwamasa, G. Y. (2006). *Culturally responsive cognitive-behavioral therapy: Assessment, practice, and supervision.* Washington, DC: American Psychological Association.

Heimberg, R. G., & Becker, R. E. (2002). *Cognitive-behavioral group therapy for social phobia: Basic mechanisms and clinical applications.* New York: Guilford Press.

Heimberg, R. G., Dodge, C. S., Hope, D. A., Kennedy, C. R., Zollo, L., & Becker, R. E. (1990). Cognitive behavioral group treatment of social phobia: Comparison to a credible placebo control. *Cognitive Therapy and Research, 14*, 1–23.

Heimberg, R. G., & Holaway, R. M. (2007). Examination of the known-groups validity of the Liebowitz Social Anxiety Scale. *Depression and Anxiety, 24*, 447–454.

Heimberg, R. G., Holt, C. S., Schneier, F. R., Spitzer, R. L., & Liebowitz, M. R. (1993). The issues of subtypes in the diagnosis of social phobia. *Journal of Anxiety Disorders, 7*, 249–269.

Heimberg, R. G., Horner, K. J., Juster, H. R., Safren, S. A., Brown, E. J., Schneier, F. R., et al. (1999). Psychometric properties of the Liebowitz Social Anxiety Scale. *Psychological Medicine, 29*, 199–212.

Heimberg, R. G., Liebowitz, M. R., Hope, D. A., Schneier, F. R., Holt, C. S., Welkowitz, L. A., et al. (1998). Cognitive behavioral group therapy vs. phenelzine therapy for social phobia: 12-week outcome. *Archives of General Psychiatry, 55,* 1133–1141.

Heimberg, R. G., Mueller, G. P., Holt, C. S., Hope, D. A., & Liebowitz, M. R. (1992). Assessment of anxiety in social interaction and being observed by others: The Social Interaction Anxiety Scale and the Social Phobia Scale. *Behavior Therapy, 23,* 53–73.

Heimberg, R. G., Salzman, D. G., Holt, C. S., & Blendell, K. A. (1993). Cognitive-behavioral group treatment for social phobia: Effectiveness at five-year followup. *Cognitive Therapy and Research, 17,* 325–339.

Heimberg, R. G., & Turk, C. L. (2002). Assessment of social phobia. In R. G. Heimberg & R. E. Becker (Eds.), *Cognitive-behavioral group therapy for social phobia: Basic mechanisms and clinical applications* (pp. 107–126). New York: Guilford Press.

Herbert, J. D., Gaudiano, B. A., Rheingold, A. A., Myers, V. H., Dalrymple, K., & Nolan, E. M. (2005). Social skills training augments the effectiveness of cognitive behavioral group therapy for social anxiety disorder. *Behavior Therapy, 36,* 125–138.

Herek, G. M. (2009). Sexual stigma and sexual prejudice in the United States: A conceptual framework. In D. A. Hope (Ed.), *Contemporary perspectives on lesbian, gay, and bisexual identities: The 54th Nebraska Symposium on Motivation* (pp. 65–111). New York: Springer.

Hirsch, C. R., & Clark, D. M. (2004). Information-processing bias in social phobia. *Clinical Psychology Review, 24,* 799–825.

Hirsch, C., Clark, D. M., & Mathews, A. (2006). Imagery and interpretations in social phobia: Support for the combined cognitive biases hypothesis. *Behavior Therapy, 37,* 223–236.

Hofmann, S. G., Newman, M. G., Becker, E., Taylor, C. B., & Roth, W. T. (1995). Social phobia with and without avoidant personality disorder: Preliminary behavior therapy outcome findings. *Journal of Anxiety Disorders, 9,* 427–438.

Holt, C. S., Heimberg, R. G., Hope, D. A., & Liebowitz, M. R. (1992). Situational domains of social phobia. *Journal of Anxiety Disorders, 6,* 63–77.

Hope, D. A. (1993). Exposure and social phobia: Assessment and treatment considerations. *The Behavior Therapist, 16,* 7–12.

Hope, D. A., Burns, J. A., Hayes, S. A., Herbert, J. A., & Warner, M. D. (2010). Automatic thoughts and cognitive restructuring in cognitive behavioral group therapy for social anxiety disorder. *Cognitive Therapy and Research, 34,* 1–12.

Hope, D. A., Heimberg, R. G., & Bruch, M. A. (1995). Dismantling cognitive- behavioral group therapy for social phobia. *Behaviour Research and Therapy, 33,* 637–650.

Hope, D. A., Heimberg, R. G., & Turk, C. L. (2010). *Managing social anxiety: A cognitive-behavioral therapy approach* (Client Workbook, 2nd ed.). Oxford: Oxford University Press.

Hope, D. A., Herbert, J. D., & White, C. (1995). Diagnostic subtype, avoidant personality disorder, and efficacy of cognitive behavioral group therapy for social phobia. *Cognitive Therapy and Research, 19,* 399–417.

Hope, D. A., Rapee, R. M., Heimberg, R. G., & Dombeck, M. (1990). Representation of the self in social phobia: Vulnerability to social threat. *Cognitive Therapy and Research, 14,* 177–189.

Human Rights Campaign. (2009). *Federal legislation: Employment nondiscrimination act.* Retrieved April 29, 2009, from http://www.hrc.org/laws_and_elections/4732.htm

Izard, C. E. (1992). Basic emotions, relations among emotions, and emotion-cognition relations. *Psychological Review, 100,* 68–90.

Katzelnick, D. J., Kobak, K., DeLeire, T., Henk, H. J., Greist, J., Davidson, J. R. T., et al. (2001). Impact of generalized social anxiety disorder in managed care. *American Journal of Psychiatry, 158,* 1999–2007.

Kendall, P. C., Chu, B., Gifford, A., Hayes, C., & Nauta, M. (1998). Breathing life into a manual: Flexibility and creativity with manual-based treatments. *Cognitive and Behavioral Practice, 5,* 177–198.

Kendall, P. C., Gosch, E., Furr, J. M., & Sood, E. (2008). Flexibility within fidelity. *Journal of American Academy of Child and Adolescent Psychiatry, 47,* 1–7.

Kessler, R. C., Berglund, P., Demler, O., Jin, R., Merikangas, K., & Walters, E. E. (2005). Lifetime prevalence and age-of-onset distributions of DSM-IV disorders in the National Comorbidity Survey Replication. *Archives of General Psychiatry, 62,* 593–602.

Kessler, R. C., Chiu, W. T., Demler, O., Merikangas, K., & Walters, E. E. (2005). Prevalence, severity, and comorbidity of 12-month DSM-IV disorders in the National Comorbidity Survey Replication. *Archives of General Psychiatry, 62,* 617–627.

Koszycki, D., Benger, M., Shlik, J., & Bradwejn, J. (2007). Randomized trial of a meditation-based stress reduction program and cognitive behavior therapy in generalized social anxiety disorder. *Behaviour Research and Therapy, 45,* 2518–2526.

Leary, M. R. (1983). A brief version of the Fear of Negative Evaluation Scale. *Personality and Social Psychology Bulletin, 9*, 371–375.

Ledley, D. R., Heimberg, R. G., Hope, D. A., Hayes, S. A., Zaider, T. I., Van Dyke, M., et al. (2009). Efficacy of a manualized and workbook-driven individual treatment for social anxiety disorder. *Behavior Therapy, 40*, 414–424.

Leung, A. W., & Heimberg, R. G. (1996). Homework compliance, perceptions of control, and outcome of cognitive-behavioral treatment for social phobia. *Behaviour Research and Therapy, 34*, 423–432.

Liddle, B. J. (1996). Therapist sexual orientation, gender, and counseling practices as they relate to ratings on helpfulness by gay and lesbian clients. *Journal of Counseling Psychology, 43*, 394–401.

Liebowitz, M. R. (1987). Social phobia. *Modern Problems in Pharmacopsychiatry, 22*, 141–173.

Liebowitz, M. R., Heimberg, R. G., Schneier, F. R., Hope, D. A., Davies, S., Holt, C. S., et al. (1999). Cognitive-behavioral group therapy versus phenelzine in social phobia: Long-term outcome. *Depression and Anxiety, 10*, 89–98.

Magee, W. J., Eaton, W. W., Wittchen, H.-U., McGonagle, K. A., & Kessler, R. C. (1996). Agoraphobia, simple phobia, and social phobia in the National Comorbidity Survey. *Archives of General Psychiatry, 53*, 159–168.

Marlatt, G. A., & Gordon, J. G. (Eds.) (1985). *Relapse prevention: Maintenance strategies in the treatment of addictive behaviors.* New York: Guilford Press.

Martell, C. R., Safren, S. A., & Prince, S. E. (2004). *Cognitive-behavioral therapies with lesbian, gay, and bisexual clients.* New York: Guilford Press.

Mattia, J. I., Heimberg, R. G., & Hope, D. A. (1993). The revised Stroop color-naming task in social phobics. *Behaviour Research and Therapy, 31*, 305–313.

Mattick, R. P., & Clarke, J. C. (1998). Development and validation of measures of social phobia scrutiny fear and social interaction anxiety. *Behaviour Research and Therapy, 36*, 455–470.

McEwan, K. L., & Devins, G. M. (1983). Is increased arousal in social anxiety noticed by others? *Journal of Abnormal Psychology, 92*, 417–421.

Mattick, R. P., Peters, L., & Clarke, J. C. (1989). Exposure and cognitive restructuring for social phobia: A controlled study. *Behavior Therapy, 20*, 3–23.

Meier, V. J., & Hope, D. A. (1998). Assessment of social skills. In A. S. Bellack & M. Hersen (Eds.), *Behavioral assessment: A practical handbook* (pp. 232–255). Needham Heights, MA: Allyn & Bacon.

Mennin, D. S., Fresco, D. M., & Heimberg, R. G. (1998, November). *Determining subtype of social phobia in session: Validation using a receiver operating characteristic (ROC) analysis.* Paper presented at the 32nd Annual Meeting of the Association for Advancement of Behavior Therapy, Washington DC.

Mennin, D. S., Fresco, D. M., Heimberg, R. G., Schneier, F. R., Davies, S. O., & Liebowitz, M. R. (2002). Screening for social anxiety disorder in the clinical setting: Using the Liebowitz Social Anxiety Scale. *Journal of Anxiety Disorders, 16,* 661–673.

Miller, W. R., & Rollnick, S. (2002). *Motivational interviewing: Preparing people for change* (2nd ed.). New York: Guilford Press.

Morgan, K. S. (1992). Caucasian lesbians' use of psychotherapy: A matter of attitude? *Psychology of Women Quarterly, 16,* 127–130.

Norton, P. J., & Hope, D. A. (2001). Kernels of truth or distorted perceptions: Self and observer ratings of social anxiety and performance. *Behavior Therapy, 32,* 765–786.

Öst, L. G. (1987). Applied relaxation: Description of a coping technique and review of controlled studies. *Behaviour Research and Therapy, 25,* 397–409.

Pachankis, J. E., & Goldfried, M. R. (2004). Clinical issues in working with lesbian, gay, and bisexual clients. *Psychotherapy: Theory, Research, Practice, Training, 41,* 227–246.

Pachankis, J. E., & Goldfried, M. R. (2006). Social anxiety in young gay men. *Journal of Anxiety Disorders, 20,* 996–1015.

Perini, S. J., Abbott, M. J., & Rapee, R. M. (2006). Perception of performance as a mediator in the relationship between social anxiety and negative post-event rumination. *Cognitive Therapy and Research, 30,* 645–659.

Persons, J. B. (1989). *Cognitive therapy in practice: A case formulation approach.* New York: W.W. Norton & Co.

Persons, J. B. (2008). *The case formulation approach to cognitive-behavioral therapy.* New York: Guilford Press.

Powers, M. B., Sigmarsson, S. R., & Emmelkamp, P. M. G. (2008). A meta-analytic review of psychological treatments for social anxiety disorder. *International Journal of Cognitive Therapy, 1,* 94–113.

Rapee, R. M., & Heimberg, R. G. (1997). A cognitive-behavioral model of anxiety in social phobia. *Behaviour Research and Therapy, 35,* 741–756.

Rapee, R. M., & Lim, L. (1992). Discrepancy between self- and observer ratings of performance in social phobics. *Journal of Abnormal Psychology*, *101*, 728–731.

Reich, J., Goldenberg, I., Vasile, R., Goisman, R., & Keller, M. (1994). A prospective follow-along study of the course of social phobia. *Psychiatry Research*, *54*, 249–258.

Rodebaugh, T. L. (2004). I might look OK, but I'm still doubtful, anxious, and avoidant: The mixed effects of enhanced video feedback on social anxiety symptoms. *Behaviour Therapy and Research*, *42*, 1435–1451.

Rodebaugh, T. L., & Chambless, D. L. (2002). The effects of video feedback on self-perception of performance: A replication and extension. *Cognitive Therapy and Research*, *26*, 629–644.

Rodebaugh, T. L., Woods, C. M., & Heimberg, R. G. (2007). The reverse of social anxiety is not always the opposite: The reverse-scored items of the Social Interaction Anxiety Scale do not belong. *Behavior Therapy*, *38*, 192–206.

Rodebaugh, T. L., Woods, C. M., Thissen, D. M., Heimberg, R. G., Chambless, D. L., & Rapee, R. M. (2004). More information from fewer questions: The factor structure and item properties of the original and Brief Fear of Negative Evaluation Scale. *Psychological Assessment*, *16*, 169–181.

Roth, D., Antony, M. M., & Swinson, R. P. (2001). Interpretations for anxiety symptoms in social phobia. *Behaviour Research and Therapy*, *39*, 129–138.

Roth, D. A., & Heimberg, R. G. (2001). Cognitive-behavioral models of social anxiety disorder. *Psychiatric Clinics of North America*, *24*, 753–771.

Ruscio, A. M., Brown, T. A., Chiu, W. T., Sareen, J., Stein, M. B., & Kessler, R. C. (2008). Social fears and social phobia in the USA: Results from the National Comorbidity Survey Replication. *Psychological Medicine*, *38*, 15–28.

Safren, S. A., Heimberg, R. G., & Juster, H. R. (1997). Client expectancies and their relationship to pretreatment symptomatology and outcome of cognitive-behavioral group treatment for social phobia. *Journal of Consulting and Clinical Psychology*, *65*, 694–698.

Schneier, F. R., Erwin, B. A., Heimberg, R. G., Marshall, R. D., & Mellman, L. (2007). Social anxiety disorder and specific phobias. In G. O. Gabbard (Ed.), *Gabbard's treatments of psychiatric disorders* (4th ed., pp. 495–506). Washington, DC: American Psychiatric Press, Inc.

Schneier, F. R., Heckelman, L. R., Garfinkel, R., Campeas, R., Fallon, B. A., Gitow, A., et al. (1994). Functional impairment in social phobia. *Journal of Clinical Psychiatry*, *55*, 322–331.

Schneier, F. R., Johnson, J., Hornig, C. D., Liebowitz, M. R., & Weissman, M. M. (1992). Social phobia: Comorbidity and morbidity in an epidemiologic sample. *Archives of General Psychiatry, 49,* 282–288.

Schultz, L. T., & Heimberg, R. G. (2008). Attentional focus in social anxiety disorder: Potential for interactive processes. *Clinical Psychology Review, 28,* 1206–1221.

Soifer, S., Zgourides, G., Himle, J., & Pickering, N. L. (2001). *Shy bladder syndrome: Your step-by-step guide to overcoming paruresis.* Oakland, CA: New Harbinger Publications, Inc.

Sposari, J. A., & Rapee, R. M. (2007). Attentional bias toward facial stimuli under conditions of social threat in socially phobic and nonclinical participants. *Cognitive Therapy and Research, 31,* 23–37.

Stangier, U., Heidenreich, T., Peitz, M., Lauterbach, W., & Clark, D. M. (2003). Cognitive therapy for social phobia: Individual versus group treatment. *Behaviour Research and Therapy, 41,* 991–1007.

Stein, M. B., Chartier, M. J., Hazen, A. L., Kozak, M. V., Tancer, M. E., Lander, S., et al. (1998). A direct interview family study of generalized social phobia. *American Journal of Psychiatry, 155,* 90–97.

Stopa, L., & Clark, D. M. (1993). Cognitive processes in social phobia. *Behaviour Research and Therapy, 31,* 255–267.

Taylor, S. (1996). Meta-analysis of cognitive-behavioral treatments for social phobia. *Journal of Behavior Therapy and Experimental Psychiatry, 27,* 1–9.

Tompkins, M. A. (2004). *Using homework in psychotherapy: Strategies, guidelines and forms.* New York: Guilford Press.

Trower, P., & Gilbert, P. (1989). New theoretical conceptions of social anxiety and social phobia. *Clinical Psychology Review, 9,* 19–35.

Turk, C. L., Lerner, J., Heimberg, R. G., & Rapee, R. M. (2001). An integrated cognitive-behavioral model of social anxiety. In S. G. Hofmann & P. M. DiBartolo (Eds.), *From social anxiety to social phobia: Multiple perspectives* (pp. 281–303). Needham Heights, MA: Allyn & Bacon.

Turner, S. M., Beidel, D. C., Dancu, C. V., & Stanley, M. A. (1989). An empirically derived inventory to measure social fears and anxiety: The Social Phobia and Anxiety Inventory. *Psychological Assessment, 1,* 35–40.

Turner, S. M., Beidel, D. C., Wolff, P. L., Spaulding, S., & Jacob, R. G. (1996). Clinical features affecting treatment outcome in social phobia. *Behaviour Research and Therapy, 34,* 795–804.

Veljaca, K., & Rapee, R. M. (1998). Detection of negative and positive audience behaviors by socially anxious subjects. *Behaviour Research and Therapy, 36,* 311–321.

Vriends, N., Becker, E. S., Meyer, A., Michael, T., & Margraf, J. (2007). Subtypes of social phobia: Are they of any use? *Journal of Anxiety Disorders, 21*, 59–75.

Walsh, K., & Hope, D. A. (2010). LGB affirmative cognitive behavioral treatment for social anxiety: A case study applying evidence-based practice principles. *Cognitive and Behavioral Practice, 17*, 56–65.

Walters, K. S., & Hope, D. A. (1998). Analysis of social behavior in individuals with social phobia and nonanxious participants using a psychobiological model. *Behavior Therapy, 29*, 387–407.

Weeks, J. W., Heimberg, R. G., Fresco, D. M., Hart, T. A., Turk, C. L., Schneier, F. R., et al. (2005). Empirical validation and psychometric evaluation of the Brief Fear of Negative Evaluation Scale in patients with social anxiety disorder. *Psychological Assessment, 17*, 179–190.

Weeks, J. W., Spokas, M. E., & Heimberg, R. G. (2007). Psychometric evaluation of the Mini-Social Phobia Inventory (Mini-SPIN) in a treatment-seeking sample. *Depression and Anxiety, 24*, 382–391.

Wegner, D. M. (1994). Ironic processes of mental control. *Psychological Review, 101*, 34–52.

Wells, A., Clark, D. M., & Ahmad, S. (1998). How do I look with my minds eye: Perspective taking in social phobic imagery. *Behaviour Research and Therapy, 36*, 631–634.

Westra, H. A., & Dozois, D. J. A. (2006). Preparing clients for cognitive behavioural therapy: A randomized pilot study of motivational interviewing for anxiety. *Cognitive Therapy and Research, 30*, 481–498.

Widiger, T. A. (1992). Generalized social phobia versus avoidant personality disorder: A commentary on three studies. *Journal of Abnormal Psychology, 101*, 340–343.

Wolpe, J., & Lazarus, A. A. (1967). *Behavior therapy techniques: A guide to the treatment of neuroses*. Oxford: Pergamon Press.

About the Authors

Debra A. Hope, PhD, received her doctoral degree in clinical psychology from the State University of New York at Albany in 1990 after completing her doctoral internship at the Medical College of Pennsylvania/Eastern Pennsylvania Psychiatric Institute. In 2003–2004 she was a scholar at the Beck Institute for Cognitive Therapy. She is currently Professor of Psychology at the University of Nebraska-Lincoln and Director of the UNL Anxiety Disorders Clinic in UNL's Psychological Consultation Center. She also serves as chair of the UNL Graduate Program in Psychology and Series Editor for the Nebraska Symposium on Motivation. Dr. Hope has published over 90 papers and books on social anxiety, cognitive-behavioral psychotherapy, social skills, and schizophrenia. Her recent work has explored the nature of social anxiety among individuals who identify as gay, lesbian, and bisexual. Dr. Hope is the 2011 President of the Association of Behavioral and Cognitive Therapies.

Richard G. Heimberg, PhD, received his degree in clinical psychology in 1977 from Florida State University. He is currently Professor and David Kipnis Distinguished Faculty Fellow at Temple University, where he also directs the Adult Anxiety Clinic. Dr. Heimberg is widely credited with the development of the cognitive-behavioral treatment for social anxiety on which this manual is based, and his treatment development research has been supported by the National Institute of Mental Health since the early 1980s. He is past President of the Association of Behavioral and Cognitive Therapies and sits on the Scientific Advisory Board of the Anxiety Disorders Association of America. He is coauthor or coeditor of eight books and over 300 papers on social anxiety disorder, other anxiety disorders, depression, as well as the practice of cognitive-behavioral therapy. Dr. Heimberg is past Editor of *Behavior Therapy*, past Associate Editor of *Cognitive Therapy and Research*, and sits on the editorial boards of 10 scientific journals in clinical psychology. He was also the inaugural recipient of the Academy of Cognitive Therapy's A.T. Beck Award for Significant and Enduring Contribution to Cognitive Therapy and the first recipient of the award as Outstanding Mentor given by the Association for Behavioral and Cognitive Therapies based on his work with over 60 doctoral and postdoctoral students in clinical psychology.

Cynthia L. Turk, PhD, received her doctoral degree in clinical psychology from Oklahoma State University in 1996 after completing her doctoral internship at the University of Mississippi/Department of Veterans Affairs Medical Centers Psychology Residency Consortium. She completed a postdoctoral fellowship at the Adult Anxiety Clinic at Temple University in 2002. She is currently Associate Professor of Psychology at Washburn University and Director of the Anxiety Clinic in Washburn University's Psychological Services Clinic. Dr. Turk has published approximately 30 journal articles and 15 chapters, primarily in the areas of social phobia and generalized anxiety disorder.